TAP INTO A DYNAMIC
SOURCE OF PERSONAL POWER:

It can spur your creative impulses, enhance your professional life, build physical and emotional strength, reduce stress, stimulate sexual passions, relieve physical ailments, and much more. Open your jewelry box and look at the gems you already own; think of the stones you love to wear; and use this one-of-a-kind practical guide to learn how to:

- identify specific gemstones and their powers
- select the stones that are right for your personality and goals
- program and cleanse each stone to maximize its effectiveness
- use and carry your stones to create harmonious alignments and vibrations
- bring out the full healing power of gemstones and use them to strengthen your immune system

Includes charts that help you choose stones to solve specific emotional problems, help you in your individual profession, protect you from different dangers, and aid you in many other ways.

STONE POWER

Originally published as STONE POWER II

DOROTHEE L. MELLA

WARNER BOOKS

A Warner Communications Company

This book was originally published under the title of *Stone Power II, The Legendary and Practical Use of Gems and Stones.*

Warner Books, Inc., 666 Fifth Avenue, New York, NY 10103

W A Warner Communications Company

Printed in the United States of America
First Warner Books Printing: January 1988
10 9 8 7 6 5 4 3

Cover photo by Bill Charles

Library of Congress Cataloging-in-Publication Data

Mella, Dorothee L.
    Stone power.

    Originally published: Stone power II. Albuquerque,
N.M. : Brotherhood of Life, c1986.
    Bibliography: p.
    1. Gems — Miscellanea. 2. Precious stones —
Miscellanea. 3. Occultism — Miscellanea. I. Title.
BF1442.P74M45   1988   133   87-20970
ISBN 0-446-38696-0 (pbk.) (U.S.A.)
    0-446-38697-9 (pbk.) (Canada)

ACKNOWLEDGMENTS

There are very special persons who have contributed to the entire ten year writings of *Stone Power*.

I would like to express fond appreciation to Teddy Keller, original editor of *Stone Power* for his creative efforts in launching this book. Many thanks also go to Katherine Cooper, Dr. Winnie Adams and Maureen Betz for their support and editorial assistance in three complete book writings for *Stone Power*.

The original artist of *Stone Power*, Anne Marie Shaw Eastburn, deserves gratitude for her unique drawings of 1975. For past and present excellent art I thank Heather Morgan Searle. To Wade Rogers and Studio Graphics, I also extend my thanks for their contributions to the new *Stone Power*. My gratitude to Ralph Genter for his excellent photographic work and also to Southwestern Minerals for loaning us the gems to be photographed.

Appreciation is also extended to those special typists through the years who have redone the script over and over. Without a team effort, *Stone Power* would not have come to be; a special thanks to Ramona.

Honor Your Stones

The Earth Is Alive.

The Earth's Gems And Stones Are Living Energies.

They Do Not Resemble You, But They Carry The Same
Living Forces As You.

To Secure You, To Protect You And To Inspire You,
They Will Give Up Their Lives.

Learn From Your Gemstones For They Will Teach You Sharing.

Caress Them, Nurture Them As Close Friends, With Loving Care.

Bless Your Gemstones, For They Are Among The
Children Of The Universe.

Dorothee L. Mella

CONTENTS

FOREWORD

In *Stone Power*, Dorothee L. Mella, a noted color specialist in nonverbal communications, takes you into the fascinating world of gems and stones.

A simple approach to a complex subject, you will find this book unique in its theories.

The subject of gems and stones as practical aids to enhance your life and increase your opportunities is clearly explained, citing many examples of what they have done for others.

You will learn to use gems and stones for your benefit, including how to select the best ones for you.

Twenty gem personality types are given, along with descriptions of the forty-eight most popular gemstones. In this book, "stone power" is simplified for easy, everyday use.

With this knowledge you will soon be helping yourself on the road to happiness, emotional security and success. Every home and office should have a copy of this book,

STONE POWER

PREFACE

If you are interested in knowing what your gems can do for you, read this book! You'll learn how a rock or gem can affect your life or even act as a support aid for a diet program. You'll gain valuable clues for analyzing personalities by the gem jewelry worn by others.

We will examine together the fascinating phenomenon of gem energy and action, both past and present, so that you can adapt these gem properties to your own individual needs, wishes, and desires. This information will be as interesting to the geologist and jeweler as to you, the person who is just discovering the world of gems and stones. It's time to open your jewelry box to see what you have; maybe an old treasure is waiting to be rediscovered.

As a little girl, when I was lonely, one of my favorite creative pastimes was to dig in the dirt. The various colored rocks and stones I found in the earth became my friends. I even collected treasures of sandwashed pebbles and shells from the beach on the occasional family outings there. On wintry, rainy days in Florida, when I was not allowed outdoors to play, I would bring out these acquired earth friends and examine them over and over again, making them one of my favorite play toys.

It wasn't until later that I discovered the earth had invested millions of years in the production of my rock toys. When studying science I learned that rocks and gems, so freely found by all of us, required time, water, sun, air, and earth to form. All forces of nature worked together as a manufacturing team to produce precious commodities of rocks and gems. Someday they may not be readily available, for we are removing them faster from the earth than they can be formed.

My recent interest in the allure of gems and stones was activated again about fifteen years ago when, as an art teacher, I was investigating the history of pigments and dyes used by earlier painters. Not only did I discover that early paints were always made from organic and mineral compounds, but also that many legends and myths surrounded the myriad uses of mined stones. This fascination led me to read and collect stories and myths concerning any gemstone. Much credit should be given to Dr. George Frederick Kunz, as well as to other authors, whose marvelous research into the legends and uses of stones inspired me to compare the ancients' beliefs and cultural applications of gems to our modern, practical applications.

In my first book, *Stone Power, The Legendary and Practical Use of Gems and Stones*, published in 1976, I attempted to simplify the folklore history of many popular stones, as well as focus the reader's attention on the effect that a favorite gemstone could have on its wearer apart from the traditional emphasis on beauty and monetary value.

In this edition of *Stone Power*, I will elaborate on the many energy uses of gems and focus on the self-help and positive uses we can derive from our common gemstones. We will explore the historical and energy values of many of your favorite gems, antique jewelry, collectibles, even your favorite rocks. We will discover how a gemstone has its own personality and how you can identify with the image each communicates. Knowledge of gem energy can be useful to you in your home or office, not only in gaining additional energy support from your jewelry, but also in enhancing your productivity.

You can experiment with the "energy feeling" of your stones. All stones are minerals with definite crystalline structures and chemical compositions. All are composed of atoms of energy. Light energy interacting with these atoms combines with the stone's chemical make-up and produces an emanating radiant energy. This you can feel. Begin recognizing this feeling by holding one stone in your left hand while closing your eyes. With practice you can become very sensitive to the different vibrations of a stone's energy. A whole new intuitive science is waiting for you. Let's begin to recognize it.

INTRODUCTION

Are you into diamonds? Gems have a way of conferring instant recognition, success, or authority. Certain individuals of history, such as Octavius Caesar, even built a reputation around a gemstone. It was said that he offered a third of the vast Roman Empire for a single opal whose power he coveted and whose beauty he wanted for his crown. The culprit gem was reported to have been owned by the Roman senator Nonius, who when exiled from Rome desired to take with him only the infamous opal. Pliny, the Roman historian, described the opal to be "as large as a hazelnut and shining with splendor to rival the colors of the Painters."

If you are a person who prefers diamonds you probably are an individualist, for a flashy display of diamonds worn on your fingers can be an effective way of demonstrating personal style, wealth, or even success. But are they really? Are diamonds a girl's or guy's best friend? Produced in the earth under tremendous heat and pressure, diamonds are carbon minerals of high thermal conductivity and have great transparency to most energy wavelengths. With these characteristics diamonds are capable of magnetizing to themselves thought vibrations and the energy of happenings. They not only may attract thought energy, but might also collect and absorb the warmth of your body. A diamond can become a powerful collector of love or psychic energy, that vibrational energy of interaction between people. Recognize the famous Hope Diamond? Could it have collected some traumatic moment that resulted in its bad luck lore? Later in this book we will explore more of the vast legends of diamonds to give us more insight into their other qualities, since they have been throughout the ages the center of intrigue, romance, love and hate, even warfare unequaled in history by any other gem.

Perhaps you never thought much about the history of the gemstones that you wear. This knowledge could be important to you, for by knowing how others have used gems, you can decide how you can make the best use of them for your benefit. Historically, gems and stones have played important roles in lifestyles. From Eastern man to the Incan, from the Crusader of Western Europe to the Egyptian Princess, these geological treasures of the earth have been valued for their practical potentials as well as for their beauty and durability.

Many articles of jewelry containing gemstones such as the blue lapis, the purple amethyst, red coral, green jade, and the orange carnelian have been found in Egyptian tombs dating back thousands of years. At least one civilization had its medicine man placing stones in open wounds to stop bleeding

15

and to speed healing. Throughout history, gems have been linked with elixirs and medicines similar to our modern pharmaceutical prescriptions. These earth treasures have been used for their hardness, or softness, and their topical healing uses: the green bloodstone with its red iron oxide content to aid blood and circulation disorders; and the yellow amber with its petrified plant carbon structure, crushed and mixed with oil prescribed as a salve, to prevent skin infections. Compare this with our penicillin or aloe creams. The ancient Orientals even cut crystals to use as correction for eye ailments. Could this have been the beginning of modern eyeglasses?

Over the centuries there have been lucky stones or unlucky stones; gems to inspire love and others to conjure hate. Power has been attributed to certain stones for affecting the mind, for attuning to the soul, for inspiring creativity, for protection, healing and much, much more.

Important religious and spiritual beliefs have included gem power. As an example of one unique spiritual property of a gemstone, there are numerous references in the Old Testament of the Bible concerning the purple amethyst. It is written that Aaron, the Jewish High Priest, wore the amethyst at the center of his breastplate, as many Jews believed that the spiritual amethyst induced visions and revelations. Again in the Christian era, a common practice was to identify a certain gem with each of the twelve apostles. St. Thomas, who traveled often by boat to different lands preaching the gospel, was identified with the blue aquamarine, a Roman gemstone that meant "sea water" by its very name, for it supposedly guaranteed safety when traveling on the sea.

Gem values have changed with changing ideas. The once prized gem of the Romans, the opal, lost its value because of a novel written by Sir Walter Scott, *Anne of Geirstein,* during the reign of Queen Victoria. The opal was portrayed to bring misfortune to its wearer or owner. Prices fell until this honored stone became practically worthless. Fortunately today the opal is sought again for its intrinsic beauty and value, and for its legendary power as a love stone.

Identity, healing, religious and spiritual significance, emotional support, and protection; all of these have been associated throughout history with the power of gemstones. This book may alter your appreciation of your personal gems. The tantalizing folklore of the stones may support your personal beliefs or begin to open you to a new understanding of how your stones can work for you. Your reward will be the greatest treasure of all: a new appreciation of life and new stone friends to support and comfort you.

Gem Values

CHAPTER
1

1
Gem Values

Through time, civilization and cultures have valued various gemstones for many different reasons. Those we know of came down to us through written records, cultural memories, legends, and because of archeological finds in all parts of the world. The use of gemstones as amulets and talismans is shown in many ancient records yet thousands of years must have already elapsed before civilization could produce even the simplest literature on gems. Before written words, the ancient Egyptians believed in the curative and protective efficiency of gems and stones. A hieroglyphic papyrus dating back nearly four thousand years described a medical treatment using a gemstone. Later in time one of the most fascinating complete therapeutic manuscripts ever discovered in Egypt was the "Papyrus Ebers," dated 1500 BC, which offered prescriptions containing gemstones and minerals.

Other stories of gem power or gem therapy were passed down through generations of families by "word of mouth." Some of the earliest texts of printed literary sources on gemstones originated from the Roman historians Pliny and Solinus. A famous, yet primitive text, on the history of gemstones, *Cysianides*, was derived from the ancient Alexandrian School of Greece. The most renowned printed work and the most copied of all early printed texts was *The History of Jewels*, by Albertus Magnus, a medieval philosopher who lived in the early 1200's. This text was to influence many of the alchemists and their research contributions on gem energy.

In ancient Egypt, stone folklore was traceable and depicted through hieroglyphics, particularly in the papyrus Book of the Dead. Some of the earliest gems were shaped into hearts and eyes. Lapis lazuli, carnelian, amber, turquoise, jade, tiger's eye, serpentine, and the chrysoberyls or eye stones were many of the gemstones uncovered in the tombs. They were used not only for personal adornment, but inlaid into amulets, shields, goblets, armors, and utensils. In tomb findings one of the images worn by the Egyptian High Priest Aelian was an eye fashioned out of lapis lazuli and ornamented with gold. This medallion represented his infallibility when speaking truths. The early Egyptians appeared to honor the "semi-precious" stones rather than the valued "precious" stones of today. Diamonds, for instance, were rare in the finds of ancient Egypt. Jade, a common gem of the Egyptians, was often used for trade and commerce, as were many other gems, for the Egyptians were one of the earliest nations to place monetary value upon the stone kingdom.

The spiritual properties of gemstones were important to the eastern civilizations of China, Tibet, and Northern India. These cultures were concerned not

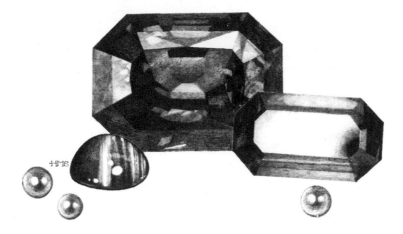

only with the medicinal and protective values of gems, but also used them for educational and spiritual enhancement. In fashioning amulets, or protective neckwear adornments, the red stones were for treating disease and protecting from fires and bad weather while the blue and violet stones were associated with virtue and faith. The yellow stones were for happiness and prosperity and the green for fertility and strength. These protective gemstones were hung about the necks of the children, not only to assure the protection from heaven but to teach them awareness and obedience to their parents. When a child was born a ceremony similar to Christian baptism was held and an astrological gem was assigned to enhance personality gifts and development. These eastern cultures, like the Egyptians, favored the lapis lazuli for wisdom, the moonstone for love, the carnelian for strength, and the turquoise for prosperity.

In early Africa, gem and stone beads were used for just about everything. They were personal ornaments worn for courage and power, for fertility rites, hunting, birth and burial; spiritual as well as practical beads were purposely used for family identity and as trading beads or currency. Dwellers of the North African deserts often plaited their hair with garlands of beads of carnelian, bits of amber, carved shell discs and colored bone talismans symbolizing their tribal inheritance as well as their family lifestyle. The more beads the women of the tribe wore the wealthier they were considered in their society. Among the popular beads were colored agates, amber, amazonite, serpentine, malachite, and lapis lazuli. Luster and color were important to the ancient Africans, for the more color the bead stone had, the more prized it was. For a millennium, African artisans fashioned ornaments of ivory which was to be valued not only for its polished texture and beauty but also for its legendary powers to heal, to protect and to honor gods and ancestral spirits. Bone and teeth beads were prized mainly as amulets for the hunt, and to call forth bravery.

Still, in another area of the world, ancient Jews were concerned with the use of gems for their symbolic properties of psychological and physical virtues. The Jewish historian Josephus reported that the gems inlaid in the breastplate of the High Jewish Priest represented love, wisdom, truth, justice, peace, equilibrium, humility, strength, faith, joy, and victory. Many students of history believe the origin of the gem breastplate is Ancient Egyptian in design.

Gemstones also symbolized Hebrew religious ideas of the Divine Glory as illustrated in the visions of the prophet Ezekiel which compared the throne of Jehovah to a sapphire; and the visions of John the Prophet of Revelations, who compared the Glory of God to multi-colored gemstones. New research indicates that the sapphire described in the Bible was actually the lapis lazuli. This most honored gemstone, named "Chesbet" by the Egyptians, was always worn by their High Priests to signify the Truth of God.

Closer to our modern times, alchemists of the early Middle Ages were fanatically concerned with the inherent healing and scientific energies of gemstones. Alchemy, though ancient in origin, dominated Western healing during the Middle Ages. Gem energies were again used for their healing properties. Some alchemists devoted themselves to the mystical sciences of transformation and transmutation of metals and matter. For example, they believed all metals had a basic essence, and by mixing an ore with a mineral, the process would transmute the metal into a higher maturity of matter. Gold was the highest product of the earth and signified perfect man. One of the major contributions of the alchemists was their work in proving the hardness of the diamond. They named the gem Adamus, the Adam of gems.

Gems and stones today are more closely identified with monetary benefits and wealth than with their inherent energy powers; countries store them in their national treasuries. Their values even exceed prices of the precious metals, platinum, gold, and silver. The Crown Jewels of the nations of Europe are some of the finest gems of the world which represent the visible emblems of royalty of all past reigning monarchs.

In England's Tower of London rests the most valuable and beautiful crown in all the world, the Imperial State Crown of Queen Victoria. Ancient gems nestle together in the crown: The 14th Century Black Prince Ruby, as large as an egg, is ringed by two huge sapphires inherited from two great former English Kings, Charles II (1630) and Edward the Confessor (1066). Rare pearl drop earrings of Queen Elizabeth and the second largest portion of the famous Star of Africa Diamond, weighing 309-3/16 carats, complete the enormous gem array. The rest of the crown is supported with a collection of 2,783 diamonds, 277 pearls, 16 sapphires, 11 emeralds and 4 rubies. Can you imagine the feeling of holding on your head such a treasury of historical wealth?

Major mining and gem areas dot the globe. We can find pearls from Japan, coral from Italy and the Philippines, turquoise from Syria and the Southwestern United States. The finest emeralds come from Colombia, South America, while the bluest lapis comes from Afghanistan. India gives us precious stones and agates, moonstones and carnelians, while Canada shares her fine amethysts and crystals with the world. African diamonds are unsurpassed, while Australia offers the finest opals; and Mexico, the rock geodes and fire agates. China and Burma are noted for their ruby and sapphire deposits, while Brazil is noted for its topaz and aquamarines. Although mining for gemstones is precarious business, since most often deposits are small and slim, we continue to hunt these precious crystals and minerals of the earth. The rarity of first class gems increases their esteem and monetary value.

The United States International Trade Commission, in the tariff schedule of "Precious Stones," lists the following: natural rubies, emeralds, diamonds, and sapphires. All the other gemstones are lumped together as "semi-precious." Earth stones such as the carnelians and agates were not mentioned. Yet, today a flawed emerald from Colombia or an imperfect ruby from China can be valued at less than a small Australian opal and can cost considerably less. L. J. Spencer, in his book *The Key to Precious Stones*, attempts to define a precious stone "as any mineral which by reason of its colors and luster is attractive in appearance, and which at the same time possesses a degree of hardness sufficient to withstand wear." Such stones are usually classified as "semi-precious" while "precious" stones are those that are rare and hard to get." For example, if the amethyst deposits of the world would suddenly become exhausted, then the amethyst gemstone would become "a precious gem" instead of what it is classified today as "a semi-precious gem."

If you would like an easy, simple memory game to discover how much your precious gems are relatively valued in today's markets, begin with the word R.E.D. A precious deep red ruby, unflawed, is the highest valued gem, followed by the emerald, and then the diamond. Then add the star gems, the blue star sapphires and the star rubies. Continue with more red and blue like the American flag, for next are red alexandrites and blue crystal sapphires from Ceylon. Opals follow; the black, the blue and the white. For the semi-precious stones, try remembering C.A.T. and P.A.T. Pat the cat, but put the cat first: C for cat's eyes, A for aquamarine, and T for topaz; P for peridot, A for amethyst, and T for tourmaline. Other gems and stones follow in their monetary value categories: lapis lazuli, turquoise, malachite, and moonstones, tiger's eyes and corals. The R stones come next, such as rhodocrosite, rhodonite and rose quartz.

Finally, end your list with a J.A.B.: J for jaspers, A for agates, and B for bloodstones, all about the same rock value. Your earth stones are the least expensive of all gemstones but they offer you enormous amounts of gem energy

A Practical Guide for Astrological Colors, Gemstones, & Metals

◆

	SIGN	COLORS	GEMSTONES*	METALS
♑	CAPRICORN January	Black and White	Onyx, Quartz, Beryl, Jet, *Garnet*, Obsidian	Gold, Silver
♒	AQUARIUS February	Electric Blue	Blue Sapphire, Lapis, Aquamarine, *Amethyst*	All Metals
♓	PISCES March	Soft Azure & Light Blue	Diamond, Turquoise, Jade, Tourmaline, *Bloodstone*	Silver
♈	ARIES April	Red-Orange	Ruby, Red Jasper, Carnelian, Coral, *Diamond*	Gold, Bronze
♉	TAURUS May	Deep Yellow to Sand Brown, or Beige	*Emerald*, Golden Topaz, Lapis, Azurite, Agate	Silver, Gold Copper
♊	GEMINI June	Violet	Crystal, Aquamarine, Alexandrite, Beryl, *Pearl*	Gold, Silver
♋	CANCER July	Green	*Ruby*, Moonstone, Pearl, Green Turquoise	Silver
♌	LEO August	Gold	Amber, Sardonyx, Ruby, Jacinth, *Peridot*	Gold
♍	VIRGO September	Purple, Deep Royal Blue	Pink Jasper, Rhodochrosite, Azurite, *Sapphire*, Star Sapphire	Gold
♎	LIBRA October	Light Yellow, Pink	*Opal*, Fire Agate, Agate, Tourmaline	All Metals
♏	SCORPIO November	Crimson	*Topaz*, Garnet, Coral, Ruby, Zircon	Gold, Silver
♐	SAGITTARIUS December	Blue-Green	Amethyst, Malachite, Zircon, *Turquoise*	Silver, Gold Copper

*The most popular association and identity of your astrological gemstone.
This concurs with the English/American birthstone charts.*

◆

from the earth. So maybe their value is really monetary after all; call it therapeutic or trade energy.

Last but not least, let us focus on the gemstone identity uses. Back to the earliest traceable societies, gemstones have been assigned as symbols of image and identity. Countries have national gems. The signs of the zodiac and the months of the year alike have gem designations, as do the planets. The Twelve Apostles had their specified corresponding stones. In another Biblical reference of revelation, the gates of the City of Jerusalem were adorned with appropriate gemstones. The histories of gem identities vary according to the authority cited, but here is some of the synthesized distillation of colors and gem identities from all of the early civilizations. Look for your birthstone identity, as a birthstone makes a wonderful gift to give yourself on your birthday or to give a friend!

Gems and Stones as Resources

CHAPTER
2

2
Gems and Stones as Resources

When you lie out in the sun, you can become sunburned. That same electromagnetic energy, sunlight, has been absorbed into rocks during their formation. High energy is present in all gemstones for they contain many components similar to our own bodies, such as light, water and minerals, but in greater density. Because of this basic identity and similarity of structure, we react to our jewelry and to stones around us. You recognize your interaction with plants. The more love and energy and care you give to them, the more energy and growth they return to you. The same with your rocks and gems. The more you wear your gems and honor them, the more they will give to you.

You'll want to be knowledgeable about colors and uses of your gemstones to enhance your image of yourself. Also, you'll want to acquire the proper energy value from your jewelry and stones, as you might honor their price tag and dollar value.

A gem's energy can be absorbed like a vitamin into our own biological system. Gemstones make us feel good, or not so good. Their energies can be soothing, securing or healing. On the other hand, they can be aggravating, irritating, and even detrimental to our peace of mind. We also can get an overdose of a stone's energy for we emotionally respond to rocks and gems just as we react to food, color, music or sound.

Opaque stones tend to produce a denser and stronger energy effect upon us than the crystalline or transparent gems. When you finger or rub a stone you absorb its energy rapidly. When you wear a gem, you slowly interact with the gem's energy as well as with any additional vibes that have collected on the gem. Think of your antique pieces of jewelry. They may contain historical energies of their former owners, of places or even of happenings; a true history book contained in their own vibratory universe.

An acquaintance of mine, a renowned nutritionist, related to me a story concerning her experience with gem energy. She had dreamed about being an early Virginia colonial lady who missed her European homeland and family. In her dream she constantly wore a favorite ring which reminded her of the "old days" before she came to America, for it was the image of a classical cameo of a fashionable French lady with elegant curls. In the dream, times were hard and it was difficult to keep her hair curled as well as clean. When my friend awakened from her dreaming, she felt that the ring that she was fantasizing about represented something about her own image and grooming today. Maybe she should curl her hair. About a week later her mother came to visit and together they went sightseeing and shopping. In a little antique shop in

Alexandria, Virginia, my friend lived her dream. Sitting on the shelf in the store was a small jewel box designed in a French motif. She picked it up to look at its pattern. Upon opening the box, to her amazement, there was a small cameo ring, with the face of a fashionable lady with elegant curls, the exact ring of her dreams. More amazing, the antique shop owner related that she felt the ring was about 200 years old according to its setting and style. My friend placed the ring on her finger, and to her growing excitement, it was a perfect fit. It was meant to be. She was meant to find her ring. The cameo ring was for her a new image, her curls and her joy. The energy of the ring made her dream become a reality. Months later, when I saw my friend again, she indeed had a new image, curly hair and a new apartment. The cameo ring, like a vitamin, with its historical energy had motivated and convinced her to change and fix up her image. The gem had become an energy motivator.

If you lose a stone or break a gem, which by the way can happen any time, it may mean that you can't tolerate the energy of that gem or stone, or you may have overused or abused its energy. Your stone can't take any more so it goes off, gets lost, or even breaks. Sometimes gemstones lose themselves or break to protect you. They will take upon themselves the stress energy that was meant for you. Historically, malachites have been known to absorb the danger directed toward their owners or wearers. The emerald has been known to crack when its owner would not listen to inner or external advice, or when its wearer could not see clearly. The sapphire used to roll away, the ruby broke in half, and the opal cracked. This energy property of a gemstone is one of the most lasting of all legends surrounding gems. It was believed that gems would give up their lives to honor the living. Have you ever lost or broken your gems? Maybe there was a reason.

Early humankind placed talismans of rocks and gems around their necks as protective amulets. Ancient peoples were aware of the protective power of stones since archeologists have found amulets, prayer beads, and gemstones of all kinds in many burial diggings, grave sites, and tombs. Often the stones were made into shields, facial masques, protective neckbands and necklaces. Protective energy by gemstones can still be the greatest power energy use for your gems. In the Mideastern countries today, traders carry eye agates and amber for protection as an aid in traveling and bargaining. Eye agates in the East were always considered protection from "the evil eye." The amber, a fossilized resin of a cone-bearing tree, fortified internal protective energies against outside stresses. Amber will also lose itself or use itself up as a misused protective aid.

There are many, many legends and examples of gemstones acting as protectors, too numerous to cite, offering protection for your mind, your body or your actions. Now take a closer look at your favorite rocks or gems and feel, by touching them, what amazing energy power they might offer to you.

In my home I place protective stones and ancient Indian rocks by my doors and windows for protection. My plants enjoy having protective stones of agates and petrified woods around their bases so no unwanted blight might invade their plant world. They seem to react to the energy of these mineral creations and grow extra healthy and strong. When you go hiking or visiting in the hills and countryside, you might want to gather some colorful stones and rocks and treat your plants to this method of protection. Remember, a stone of nature has a good light energy, and you will feel and react to the right ones for your personal needs of protection.

Gem and Stone Personality

CHAPTER
3

3
Gem and Stone Personality

What would you be if you could be a gemstone? This may seem to be an unusual question at first. Think about it for a moment. The answer is bound to tell you something about yourself. Most of us have played the game, "If I could be a color, I would be a _____", or "If I could be an animal, I would be a _____."

These behavior modification associations can always help identify some of your personal qualities and strong characteristics. A gemstone identity association will do the same thing, for like you, a gem has specific identities.

Once you've decided what gemstone you are, it will be fun to ask the same question of your spouse, close friends, even your boss, or any person that has an influence in your life. You may discover characteristics of that person. You can also recognize areas in which you and your associate could use positive reinforcement. You'll get "sure fire" gift ideas for family and friends.

Try experimenting with carrying your identity stone to strengthen your personality and to reflect your wealth and value of yourself.

Below are listed 20 stones for your personal identity, followed by a personality description of the individual stone. By noting a new choice, you may even become more aware of changes in your outlook. Like a gemstone, be more open to light and yourself. Pick from the list below first, and then look up your preferred stone on the pages that follow.

1. Agate	11. Malachite
2. Amber	12. Moonstone
3. Amethyst	13. Opal
4. Aquamarine	14. Pearl
5. Crystal	15. Petrified Wood
6. Diamond	16. Ruby
7. Emerald	17. Sapphire
8. Garnet	18. Topaz
9. Jade	19. Tiger's Eye
10. Lapis Lazuli	20. Turquoise

Pick only your identity stone and read about its complement.

AGATE

You are many colors, in fact, almost any color. You give people security and you protect them. You are energetic. As an agate personality, you are able to work well with the earth, for you are a good organizer, simplistic and stable.

You like to have rainbows around you because you are very communicative. You are able to talk to most people. Wear multi-colored agates for additional strength to carry out your goals.

Your complement is a *lapis lazuli.* Lapis stimulates your intellect. It brings wisdom to your organizational energies.

AMBER

As an amber, you identify with life and growing life forms. You are golden in color or ruby red. You have a very warm, sensitive nature, and, in turn, you make a strong protector for other sensitive people. You love nature. You are loving and down to earth, although your personality is not as secure as an agate personality.

Your complement is a *crystal.* A crystal reflects all light and will introduce you to new ways of doing things. It can help you to become more open to your body needs, and in turn, more physically healthy.

AMETHYST

An amethyst person is very spiritual and thoughtful. You look for higher values, rather than for practical things. You are a regal, purple color. You are intuitive and sensitive as well as spiritual. As an amethyst, you help others to get in touch with their faith. Sometimes it is hard to tell you what to do, for you know already what you want.

Your complement is an *agate.* Agates will bring you down to earth.

AQUAMARINE

You are a pale crystalline blue. As an aquamarine, you are fluid, imaginative, and fanciful. At times, you are a little self-focused, but you are good for people who are too heavy, too strong, or too forceful. You are the water. You can soothe, protect, and calm.

Your complement is *topaz.* Topaz represents the sun and can influence your water temperature and motivation.

CRYSTAL

You reflect all light. You are every color of the rainbow all at the same time. Because of this, you can relate to all peoples. You are able to energize and yet to balance and control all forms of energy. As a crystal, you are a natural healer and a humanitarian. Your focus, or sun energy, can be directed in any manner you choose.

Your complement is *petrified wood.* Petrified wood can help replenish your drained energy since you never know when to stop.

DIAMOND

You have chosen the flashiest, and the hardest, of all stones with which to identify. You are sometimes a person who carries your bankbook in your pocket. At other times, you're not always thoughtful or sensitive to others, as much as you are to your own self. You like grandeur, richness, and material power. When directed by light, you have a strong sense of inner security and purpose. You sparkle like no other gem.

Your complement is a *pearl.* A pearl can add soft earthiness to your diamond hardness.

EMERALD

You, the blue-green emerald, are insightful and universally oriented. You are always looking for the higher and lower, the left and the right, future and past, combined as one. You are a regal green crystal. You like to see far and wide. You stimulate all forms of creativity, even your own creative expressions, and are a source of strength to the arts.

Your complement is *opal.* Because you analyze clearly, an opal can help you act humanistically upon what you see.

GARNET

You are usually a deep red color that sociably combines with most other gems. As a garnet personality you are considerate and sensitive to what is going on outside yourself. You like to help others become more flexible and caring. You are solid in inner security, therefore you are supportive to the needy. Because of your ability to communicate well, you can mix and match with all types of personalities. You are everyone's friend.

Your complement is a *turquoise.* The blue-green turquoise calms your emotions and mind. It will always soothe you.

JADE

You are extremely flexible. You appear in a variety of colors, from pink to hunter green. You are elegant, and you like the life that happens at night. Because you are practical, you make good business deals. Some people call you a healer, some call you a dealer. As a dealer, you can see clearly into most situations. This ability helps you make wise business decisions.

Your complement is a *carnelian.* A carnelian adds a little security to your flexibility. It will also provide you with more focused goals.

LAPIS LAZULI

You are a beautiful royal blue gem. As a lapis lazuli you represent universal wisdom. You like to make decisions that are good for people. You have good executive qualities as long as you do not have too many fixed ideas. You are a natural politician and leader. You like your mind to be stimulated rather than your emotions, but you need to be wise about your own needs.

Your complement is a *blue lace agate.* This light blue stone will help you to relax your heavy mind.

MALACHITE

As a malachite personality, you have a very strong and forceful image. You are usually bright Kelly green in color with designs of stripes and circles. Your protection always surrounds sensitive people, as well as those who are less fortunate than you. You are good at interpretation or synthesis. You get right to the point. You see correctly. You occasionally have the habit of putting it "out there," for you like to speak your mind.

Your complement is *ivory.* This white organic stone will serve to recharge your physical batteries.

MOONSTONE

You love being a moonstone because you are a fluid, beautiful white or pink hued stone. You are the color of the moon; you attract water. Your heart and your emotions are your strength, as you stimulate love for yourself, and for others. You are love. You may find that your weakness is not knowing when to turn a deaf ear to your emotionally draining friends.

Your complement is a *lapis lazuli.* The blue lapis will put your heart in touch with your mind, and will help you to be wise.

OPAL

Because you are a combination of the moonstone and the crystal, you reflect all light from the sun and from the rainbow. Yet you have the gentleness of the moonstone. You are a humanitarian and patron. You do not mix well with people who are not of like mind, especially pessimists. You like to be positive in life. You like to shine your light.

Your complement is a *peridot.* This olive green gem will protect your gentleness and sensitivity.

PEARL

You are feminine, sensitive, cherishing, loving, sometimes too bashful. You are very securing and supportive, therefore the people around you identify you as the universal Mother or Nurturer. You can be pink, blue, or creamy with pink and blue lusters. You always are a lady. You always say the right thing. Men give you as a gift to express their love.

Your complement is *jade.* This green outgoing stone will help you think before you give, and will make you more assertive and practical.

PETRIFIED WOOD

You are very secure - an old tree turned to stone. You help people to find direction. They see you as a rock of security, or strength. You are very hard. A lot of executives identify with your "lean upon me" properties. Your color ranges from rust to yellow, to all shades of brown. You are earth, a part of earth to identify with and recognize its history.

Your complement is an *aquamarine.* This blue crystalline gem will make you a little more imaginative, a little more creative, and more fanciful in your life.

RUBY

A ruby personality is a rich, rich red; the color of strawberries or the color of wine. You have the wisdom of the King, and the beauty of the Queen of Gems. Your heart and mind are well balanced. These traits make you enjoy a position of authority where you can use your mind, your heart, and your body in your work. You like to be beautiful.

Your complement is an *emerald.* The perfect mate for a ruby, it stimulates your insight for good leadership.

SAPPHIRE

A sapphire's personality has a high mission. Your color is a royal blue. Sometimes you are so dark, you are called indigo; sometimes so light, you are called cornflower blue. You can be a star or a crystal. Being very wise, you are a good judge of character. People respect you for your mind and your wisdom. But you are not always sensitive to the needs of your own heart. Yet, you are a gem who knows that you have a destiny.

Your complements are *opal* or *moonstone.* Either one of these gems expands your awareness to your own sensitivities.

TOPAZ

You, the topaz, are crystalline energy. Most often you are the color of and shine like the sun, but you can also be pink or blue, like the sunset. You are warm and loving, and people seek you out for your abilities as a natural communicator. Sometimes, though, you talk without thinking, for you always like to be heard. You like to give energy to others.

Your complement is an *amethyst.* This purple gem can add spiritual insight to your communications.

TIGER'S EYE

As a tiger's eye, you can see everything. You are emotional and sensitive as well as insightful. You understand how things fit together in their proper order. From working a puzzle, to organizing a business, you are a good problem solver. Being a rich brown color, you always bring everything down to earth to be understood.

Your complement is a *pearl.* This gem will add softness and sensitivity to your visionary strength.

TURQUOISE

You are a beautiful blue stone, yet you can range from green to the palest sky blue. You are lucky in love and fortune. You have the ability to relax your mind in order to see more clearly. You are a good trader as you are sensitive to a good bargain. When in love, you show your colors.

Your complements are *shells.* Any shell will help to support you physically when you run out of energy.

Healing Properties
of Gemstones

CHAPTER
4

4
Healing Properties of Gemstones

Have you ever opened your jewelry box or drawer and wondered what stone to wear for the day to help support yourself? Perhaps you have bought a new ring or gem bead necklace because it felt right. Then your curiosity on what your new purchase could do for you made you wonder, "Do stones have healing energy and balancing powers?" Some of you have already experimented with amethysts to help you meditate; some of you have heard that crystals are all-around healers; and some of you have purchased lapis lazuli rings to help develop your higher minds.

Without realizing it, you have begun a new understanding of gems from which you will gain much. Moreover, the joy of discovering something new about your gemstones will not be forgotten. You will be able to use your gems for many different purposes and discover a brand new self-help aid within your stones.

For example, suppose you want to diet. You may be interested in a stone or gem that could support your self-discipline and give you additional energy while dieting.

If you're the type of person who is concerned with having a beautiful physical image, but who has little patience and some difficulty with self-discipline in following a diet, you may need some strong energy to help. Begin by putting away all your favorite "flashy" gemstones. Try some new energy support stones. Select an earth agate or a jasper, a garnet or a malachite, or even a bloodstone. They will secure your strength as you are beautifying yourself. They'll not over-stimulate your desire for food, but will aid your energy while you're disciplining yourself. Avoid your expensive diamonds and sapphires. Remove your lapis lazuli or chrysocolla and cover up your crystals. Be not only secure with your diet plan, but mentally relaxed and calm while you're obtaining your fantastic new image. Shine later when you are lighter.

If you happen to be one of those persons forever on a diet who never seems to lose much poundage, it could be that you're using your heart too much and not your head. You probably need to instruct your mind. Put away your loving opals, moonstones, and crystals. You might select a tiger's eye or a sodalite, some jade or even a jasper, or maybe some turquoise to help. You can use onyx of all colors to give additional protection to your ever giving, yet sensitive, emotional nature. Jaspers will lend support to your emotions as well as your body, while sodalite can support a positive attitude. Turquoise can calm you while a piece of jade will help you to be more practical and to eat the right foods and stay on the diet. If you're a person who is a number one escape artist on any diet, you always find an excuse for why you can't follow a discipline. You too can use gemstones for additional strength. Select moss agates, some coral or some shells. Amber is a wonderful organic stone for a diet since it supports our energy strength. Don't wear an amethyst or your favorite sapphires; these gems could encourage you to make more excuses. The earth stones will help you better.

Finally, jaspers and agates are most often considered the all-around good diet stones. Jaspers can aid you physically by their color: red, orange, brown and green, and by their compact, dense energy. Agates can help you feel secure, as they are the natural earth stones.

Dr. William T. Fernie, M.D., reported in his book, *The Occult and Curative Powers of Precious Stones*, that Galen, the noted Roman physician, honored jasper. Galen reported that the Egyptian king, Nechepsus, wore a green jasper cut in the shape of a dragon over the region of his digestive organs and indeed, it was wonderfully strengthening to their functions. Jaspers were adopted by early physicians as the most powerful astringents, regulators of metabolism and colic, and strengtheners of the stomach and digestive organs. Galen, himself, was known to wear a most favorite ring of jasper.

When you're dieting don't forget gemstones as an addition to your wardrobe, for they can give you all-around energy support.

The Creative Wellness Program in northern Virginia, run by NIMO Systems, Inc., uses certain colors in wardrobes to aid physical stamina and balance while dieting. The Creative Wellness Program also recommends the use of gems and stones as balancing aids while the clients are actively following out their diet disciplines.

The results are amazing. Mixing and matching gems to personality characteristics is helping all to become successful. These earth products are one more supportive aid for self-beautification and health. You recognize that fresh vegetables are healthy for you, for they contain many minerals and vitamins. Don't neglect the hidden health property of a stone; it too is a mineral. By the absorption of its energy into your body, it can become a natural healer, too.

In ancient days gemstones were worn often for the maintenance of health and for the cure of disease. As an external treatment, they were applied directly to various parts of the body, even into wounds to stimulate topical healing. For internal treatment, gems were often ground into powders and administered by mouth. This is not a common practice today since many minerals are poisonous. There are few natural homeopathic physicians around the world still experimenting with this method of "gem treatment," yet in areas of India and the Middle East, there exist some wise healers and spiritual teachers using gems as a "dipping mineral treatment." A gem is dipped and soaked in drinking water for a period of time, and then the water is given to the patient for a timed administration treatment. An exchange of energy occurs between the stone and the water, similar to the chlorination of our swimming pools. At times, the water even tastes like the gem itself, so strong is the energy exchange. Most miners recognize this mineral exchange with water, as water absorbs the minerals from the surrounding rock formations just flowing over or through them. Think of the mineralized water that we drink today.

About the time I began collecting data on the history of colors and gems and their amazing curative powers, a friend of mine called me with an emergency. "My son is very ill with tonsillitis and fever," she worriedly whispered on the phone. "Is there any stone in your collected materials that can aid his body during its battle with infection?" Sorting back through my materials, I came across the plant agates, specifically the moss and the tree agates which had folklore tradition of having been used by medicine men and ancient physicians as stones of choice for reduction of fevers and detoxification of the body. I offered this information to her with the encouraging advice of calling her pediatrician, then hung up.

Later, that same week, she called back, this time far more relaxed because her son was recovering. She had an amazing incident concerning a stone. She had found a small tree agate, a white stone with fossilized green plant life within, in her husband's rock collection. She washed the stone carefully and then weighed it on her kitchen food gram scale with the thought of not wanting it to be too heavy so as not to awaken him while he was sleeping. I do not remember the exact weight or gram count, but what I do recall was her amazement as to what happened physically to her tree agate. Using some non-sticky tape, she had taped the stone on the child's neck over the throat region during his nap. The agate remained there for three hours and did not seem to bother the little boy's rest. When he awoke she removed the stone to wash it again. She was pleased at his apparent improvement; he seemed less fretful with fever. Before she returned the stone to the rock collection, and before she rewashed it, she thought she would weigh it again to jot down its weight in case she wanted to reuse it. My friend couldn't believe what had transpired. The tree agate had doubled in weight yet it appeared to be the same size as before. It must have exchanged or absorbed energy, for it was indeed heavier. What had happened? Had it interchanged its energy with her son's fever or infection? We don't really know the interactive powers of gems and stones, yet something had occurred between the tree agate and her son.

There are many other stories I could share with you concerning amazing interactions of stones with human beings, and their supportive curative powers. I, myself, have been helped more than I even like to admit by the gemstone kingdom.

In the charts that follow on Gems and Stones as health balancing aids, I want to acknowledge credit to Rev. Michelle Lusson, c/o Creative Wellness, Vienna, Virginia, who willingly shared her research information with me concerning the basic healing properties of stones.

Gems and Stones as Health Balancing Aids

AGATES	contribute to physical balance
Banded	attracts strength
Blue Lace	balances body fluids
Carnelian	increases energy levels
Dendrite	elevates blood sugar level
Eye	protects from bodily harm
India	gives physical strength
Lace	relaxes muscular tensions and spasms
Moss-green	detoxifies the blood
Moss-red	purifies the blood
Plume	strengthens the veins
Tree	reduces fevers and toxins
ALEXANDRITE	stimulates sexual powers

AMAZONITE	regulates thinking faculties
AMBER	reduces fluid retention and helps to detoxify the urinary system
AMETHYST	relieves headaches
AQUAMARINE	aids eyesight and reduces fluid retention
BLOODSTONE	stimulates the flow of energy for all healing; combats physical trauma; stimulates blood circulation and stops hemorrhaging
CAT'S EYE and TIGER'S EYE	reduce headaches and nervous spasms
COPPERSTONES and GEMS	
Azurite	gives symptomatic relief of arthritis and joint disabilities; reduces hip joint pain
Chrysocolla	tranquilizes nervous tension
Malachite	prevents infection; aids fertility
Turquoise	relaxes the body
CORAL	relieves throat and voice ailments; balances physical endurance
CRYSTALS	are all-around healers
Pink Quartz	promotes skin rejuvenation
Yellow Quartz or Citrine	aids assimilation of foods
DIAMOND	has no healing properties
EMERALD	aids neurological diseases
GARNET	balances thyroid disorders
IVORY	protects the physical body from injury
JADES	promote healing of vital organs
Green Jade	comforts stomach disorders, eases eyestrain and aids liver function
Red Jade	combats female disorders, particularly the ovarian and uterine functions
JASPERS	promote healing of gastric system and balance endocrine functioning
Brown Jasper	aids female hormonal functions
Green Jasper	aids intestinal functions and reduces constipation; reduces intestinal spasms; combats ulcers
Red Jasper	balances gastric and pancreatic disorders

LAPIS LAZULI	strengthens the physical body during spiritual awakening
MOONSTONE	regulates the pituitary gland function
OBSIDIAN	boosts immunity
ONYX and SARDONYX	assist physical coordination
OPAL	increases the assimilation of protein
PEARL	promotes antibodies and fights infection
PERIDOT	aids adrenal function
PETRIFIED WOOD	restores physical energy; helps hip and back problems
RHODOCHROSITE	prevents mental breakdowns; balances physical and emotional trauma; a rescue stone
RHODONITE	restores physical energy, especially following trauma or shock; another rescue stone
RHYOLITE	rejuvenates physical beauty
RUBY	prevents schizophrenia
SAPPHIRE	increases level of potassium, magnesium and calcium
SODALITE	promotes a balance in thyroid metabolism
TOPAZ	fights kidney and bladder ailments
TOURMALINE	prevents lymphatic diseases; battles anemia
ZIRCON	like crystals, is an all-around healer

THE THREE
  MAJOR ORES

Copper	improves glandular functions
Gold	stimulates the body's electrical impulses
Silver	balances the central nerve network

Examples of Gemstones for
Maintenance of Beauty, Wellness and Balance

If you want to be energetic, motivated, dynamic, beautiful, and
socially accepted, think of the *rose* and *red* stones. Be positive!

ROSE JASPER	RHYOLITE	CARNELIAN
GARNET	**ENERGY AND BEAUTY**	RUBY
RED CORAL	ALEXANDRITE	RED JASPER

When you're tired, over-worked, and under stress, get back
to the *earth*, and wear some earth stones.

TREE AGATE		BANDED AGATE
SARD	**STRESS FREEDOM**	AMBER
SODALITE	TURQUOISE	SARDONYX

When you need to make a decision, aid your mind by
using a *green* or *blue* stone.

BLUE TOURMALINE		BLUE LACE AGATE
AZURITE	**DECISIONS MADE**	SAPPHIRE
AVENTURINE	LAPIS LAZULI	CHRYSOCOLLA

If you want a new career, new work, or even a new job, and want to
have purpose in your life, go for it with a *new support stone.*

BLUE SAPPHIRE	PLUME AGATE	STAR SAPPHIRE
GARNET	**NEW OPPORTUNITIES**	CARNELIAN
TOURMALATED QUARTZ		RUTILATED QUARTZ

How to Wear
Your Gemstones

CHAPTER
5

5

How to Wear Your Gemstones

Every object, animate or inanimate, is surrounded by its own energy field. The truly charismatic person fills a hall with her or his personality, yet an ant may radiate energy in such a way that only another ant can sense it. When you are within a three foot range of a gemstone, you are within its field-of-energy influence. A business person could keep a stone on the corner of a desk, while an artist may perch a gem on the edge of an easel, or tuck one into a paint box. Stones can be placed in lunch boxes or briefcases. Business women can keep their stones in their purses. But the most popular use for stones is to wear them. When adornment becomes more than beauty-enhancing, you are achieving two purposes with one stone.

Have you ever thought about where gems should be worn on your body? Now is the time to learn what parts of your body receive the most beneficial energy results from your jewelry.

Consider the left side of your body, your left arm, your left hand and your fingers. Your entire left side is the most sensitive side of your body. It receives energy from outside of yourself. Do you know that through your left side external influences act more quickly upon your personality? When you wear certain gems on your left side you can consciously control and modify stresses from your environment. On the other hand, when you wear gems on your right side, your gems can aid your productivity. Call your right side your doer or action side of self.

Rings of every shape and size imaginable are the most common form of gem jewelry. Let your hands be the most expressive part of your body. Your left hand, your sensor, listens and receives, while your right hand, your power hand, will direct and conduct your non-verbal expressions.

Your fingers are not merely handy digits used to push buttons or to balance cocktails; each finger has its individual purpose. You should consider where to wear a ring, and which gem on which finger.

Don't wear a ring on your thumb, for your thumb likes to be free as does your will and shouldn't be blocked.

Your pointer fingers are your directional fingers of expression and a gem on these can influence your communications, goals, dreams, and desires. On your left, stones aid toward receiving inner communications. On your right, stones can assist in sharing their energy towards your directed actions.

Your middle finger is your intuitive and inspirational finger. Only cover your middle fingers with gemstones when you want to stimulate your intuition.

Your fourth finger, or commonly called your ring finger, is your creative finger. On your left, this finger can receive all forms of creative stimulation, even love. On the fourth finger of your left hand you wear your engagement diamond or wedding ring. Not by chance, for do you know that this finger sends vibes straight to your heart?

Your little finger is your finger of change or opportunity. A gem on your left little finger can aid you in accepting changes, while the proper stone on your right little finger can influence change of your fortune or goals.

There are, of course, varied gemstones for all of your fingers, according to your personal likes and dislikes. You can match each finger with a wish stone that enhances your actions or their return, bringing you a new romance, love, wealth and success. Use your imagination and intuition to find what might work best for you. Some of the most popular action stones for finger use to aid and influence personal wishes and desires are listed on the following list.

1. Directional stones for your **POINTER** or **INDEX** fingers:

    Lapis Lazuli to stimulate personal wisdom or knowledge.
    Shells, Mother of Pearl, Garnet, and Moonstone to stimulate love of self and of humanity.
    Carnelian to stimulate your goals, actions or achievements.
    Turquoise, Sodalite, and Chrysocolla to calm and relax you.

2. Intuitive stones for your **MIDDLE** fingers:

    Amethyst to stimulate your creativity and inspirations.
    Crystals and Sapphire to inspire higher goals and directions.
    Ruby to enhance self beauty.

3. Creative stones for the **RING** fingers:

    Ruby to enhance a beautiful countenance.
    Diamond to enhance love ties.
    Emerald to stimulate creativity and new ideas.
    Tiger's Eye and Cat's Eye to focus creative insights in their proper directions.
    Moonstone to express love and love shared.
    Turquoise to combine your intuition with your practicality.
    Opal to stimulate your humanitarian goals and actions.

4. Change agent stones for your **LITTLE** fingers:
    Pearls to stimulate better organizational habits.
    Turquoise to relax your mind and nervous energy.
    Aventurine to bring to you new opportunities.

Historically, gemstones were often used as natural batteries to replenish energy. Ancient medicine men carried pouches of healing stones which were all strong energy earth stones. Crystalline gems, such as rubies, sapphires, emeralds and tourmalines, were used as generators of beauty, love, wisdom and many self-enhancing attributes.

HAND
M·A·P

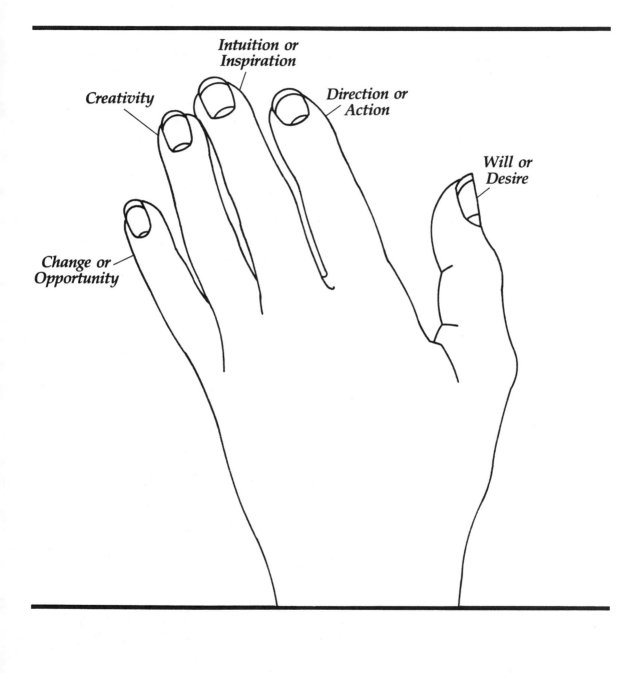

Intuition or
Inspiration

Creativity

Direction or
Action

Will or
Desire

Change or
Opportunity

You may have already discovered that you're one of those people who just can't wear a digital watch on your wrist. This may be due to the quartz in your watch reacting to your body rhythms. Don't wear it! Rather, when buying jewelry for your wrists, look for a watch or gem that can protect you, or for a bracelet of gems that can help you to release stress. Bracelets or cufflinks made of stones, such as turquoise, coral or various shells, can be particularly helpful to you to aid in the releasing of built-up energy. They can calm you when you wear them on your wrists.

Ancient warriors wore upper arm-bands studded with gems and stones to identify and support their rank, courage and strength. It is not a common practice today to wear a gemstone arm-band, but if you want to wear a gem on your upper arm, do so, for it can only have a beneficial result to your physique.

Gemstones that you wear around your neck generally affect your personality. Performance and positive self-image stones are especially good for neck jewelry. Pearls around your neck, for example, can help to build your self-image.

Regardless of whether your ears are pierced or not, gemstones on the ear usually have a beneficial effect to your body, but opals and lapis are two stones whose energy might be too high to be worn on your ears. They can sometimes cause spaciness or dizziness. Ancient Egyptian priests ground malachite to wear as eye shadow because they believed it to be a high energy stone to help them have visionary powers. But malachite is also not the best ear stone for everyone. Two good rejuvenation stones to wear on your ears are the tiger's eye and jade. Rose quartz can help you prevent wrinkles. There are many gemstones that when worn on the ears can give you a positive effect whether to support your mental keenness or perception, or to aid love. Sapphire, for example, can stimulate your wisdom, while garnet, your social acceptance.

There are, of course, jewelled hair clips for your hair, and crowns for your head containing stones that may have beautifying uses, but remember to adorn your head with gemstones that have a clear positive effect upon your growth as well as personality development.

Ancient cultures frequently practiced placing gems and stones in the center of one's forehead to increase psychic powers. This is often a favorite experiment of beginners in self-developmental studies. Unless done with caution, the results can be debilitating. Remember your forehead is the midpoint of the frontal lobes of your brain, and a gem or stone on your forehead won't do it. Greek Vestal Virgins were taught to be psychic and hear inner voices by listening to a seashell, while Lamas were taught to stare at a flame to open their powers. Rather, you might try meditating with an amethyst in your hand to increase your intuitive sensitivities.

Jewelled belts and buckles can affect your vitality and feelings of well-being. Consider the turquoise belt buckles of the Southwest: beautiful as well as functional. These stones at your waist can energize or relax you. In belt buckles, try a carnelian for motivation, agates for increased energy, a bloodstone for healing, shells or jasper for balance. Crystalline stones are better worn around

BODY
M·A·P

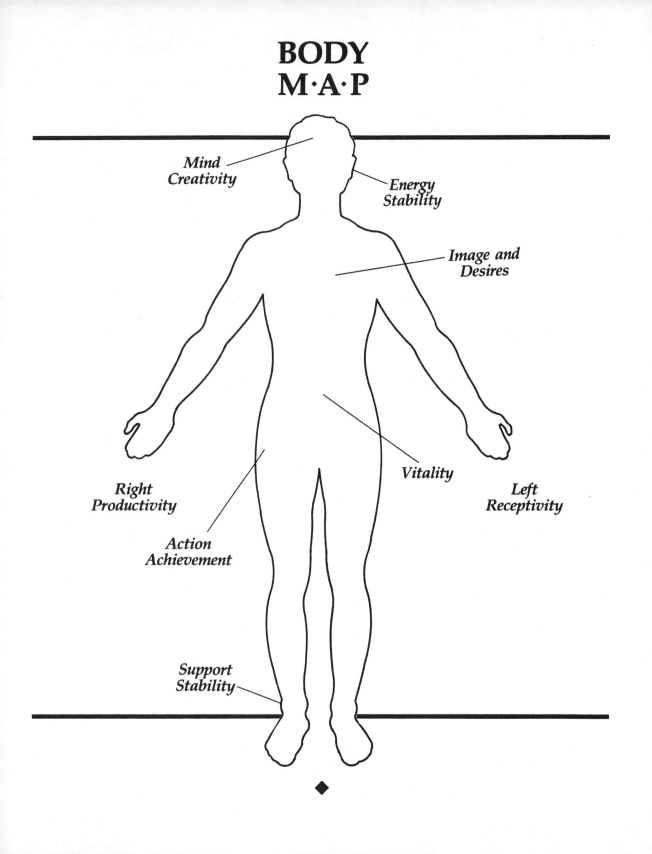

Mind
Creativity

Energy
Stability

Image and
Desires

Right
Productivity

Vitality

Left
Receptivity

Action
Achievement

Support
Stability

◆

your neck or your fingers for their own safety. Folklore states that when red coral was worn on the waist, it had a good influence upon the wearer's breathing and lungs. According to another legend, bloodstones worn on your waist can help your heart and circulation.

Stones carried in your hip pockets can influence any of your actions. For example, if you are trying to find a job, you might want a success stone that is not visible. Hide a stone in your pocket. You can also carry it in your purse or in your briefcase. Try carrying a tourmalated quartz or tourmaline for a new job. If that doesn't work, try a tiger's eye, a carnelian or a red moss agate. If you're looking for a lover, how about a moonstone in your pocket or purse? Hip and pocket stones always act as special help for almost anything.

In some cultures both men and women wear stones around their ankles to provide physical support. Ankle stones can be good supportive stones for problems such as drug or alcohol addiction, or for those who have wandered too far into the occult or psychic. Try a crystal, jasper or rhodonite. You can even place them in or on your shoes. They can ground you, erase spaciness or dizziness, and even guide you back to reality.

Learning to Identify
Your Stones

CHAPTER
6

6
Learning to Identify Your Stones

You can identify your gems and stones in many ways. Gemologists and rock hounds usually classify them by their properties of hardness, color, luster and transparency.

Color is the most apparent and most striking property in any good gemstone, yet the color of the stone is not always constant, for color can vary in many types of crystalline or mineral stones. For example, you identify a ruby, a corundum crystal gem, as red, yet some rubies are so dark, they appear purple red, and some so light, they can appear pink or orange. Turquoise, a copper stone, is usually considered blue, but depending upon its amount of mineralization, this stone can be green, yellow or even brown.

Luster is the amount and type of reflection and refraction of light by or from a gemstone. Most of us are not familiar with the luster of gems as we think all gems shine alike, but the amount of luster radiating from a gemstone is instrumental in determining the finer quality of a gem's surface.

Transparency of gems refers to a stone's ability to permit light to pass through it clearly. Often a gemstone is considered transparent if writing can be read through it, but translucent when this see-through ability is diminished by inclusions or impurities. Opaque stones are those rocks that do not let light pass through, or may exhibit a dull luster, like the turquoise or lapis.

Hardness is another main identifying property of stones, for gems must, to a certain extent, be indestructible and resist wear. The Mohs scale is the method used in determining the hardness of stones. It exhibits the resistance to scratching of the surface of a gemstone. This is important because the harder the rock, the higher the polish one gets. The scale begins with talc, like powder, #1, and ends with the hardest stone, a diamond, #10. An agate is #7 hardness and turquoise, about #4-5. Amber is a #2.5 to #3, while a ruby is #9. You can always ask your jeweler what the hardness is of the stone you're buying, or just ask for a knife blade or scratch test. If the scratch leaves a mark, the stone is below #5.5. Remember, in setting any stone with a hardness of #4 and below, care must be taken in order not to damage the gem.

Mohs Scale of Hardness for Common Stones

1-3: Soft   4-6: Medium   7-10: Hard

SOFT
1. Talc or Turquoise foam
2. Bone or Alabaster
3. Amber or Pearl

	4. Serpentine or Rhodochrosite
MEDIUM	5. Turquoise or Opal
	6. Moonstone or Lapis Lazuli
	7. Quartz or Agates (Most common gemstone hardness)
HARD	8. Topaz or Alexandrite
	9. Sapphire, Ruby, or Emerald
	10. Diamond

The rarer stones, such as rubies, diamonds, emeralds, and sapphires, we consider precious gems or stones of finer qualities. The value placed upon the precious stones and some other gems is often in proportion to the stones' fineness, brilliance, supply and fashion demand.

Whether a rock or crystal, a precious or semi-precious stone, the value to you, potential jewel wearer, should always be determined by your own personal taste, and what your gem can do for you.

In the next chapter you will find descriptions, histories and legends of most of your favorite stones. To help you understand the language of stone descriptions, I have defined some of the general terminology.

AMULET - a protective object or stone worn to ward off evil; a charm.

CABOCHON GEM - a dome cut and polished stone of various small sizes, with a flat bottom; usually translucent or opaque stones.

EARTHSTONE - a stone found on the earth's surface consisting of common earth soil or a mineral formation.

FACETED GEM - usually a crystalline gemstone cut into small flat surfaces called facets with a mirror-like bottom; this particular type of cut increases the brilliance of the stone.

GEM - a stone fashioned to bring out its beauty in order to be used in jewelry.

GEMSTONE - a stone cut or faceted in a manner in order to be used for adornment.

MINERAL - any class of substances occurring in nature usually comprising inorganic substances of definite chemical composition and definite crystal structure.

ORE - a metal-bearing mineral or rock, or a native metal valued enough to be mined.

ROCK - a mass of stone or mineral matter of various compositions consolidated or unconsolidated by the action of heat or water.

RUBBING STONE - a smooth stone naturally polished by nature and used by man as a stone for hand pressure and friction.

SPECIMEN - a part exemplifying a whole mass of rock or any various mineral composites.

STONE - a piece or particular kind of rock which is composed of the hard substance of which rocks consist.

TALISMAN - a stone or object engraved with characters believed to possess mystical powers which is worn as an amulet or charm.

A to Z of Stone Power

CHAPTER
7

Rhodonite

Pearl

Botswana Agate

Opal

Cat's Eye

Jasper

Red Amber

Turquoise

Rose Quartz

Malachite

Amber

Rutile Quartz

Bluelace Agate

Moonstone

Lapis Lazuli

Jade

7

A to Z of Stone Power

To give you an introduction to this index of gems and stones from A to Z of the most popular gem minerals is most important!

We will take each stone separately as a member of the rock kingdom and reference will be made to its folklore, legend and history of practical applications. Some of you may find this information dry, but some of you will certainly look up your favorite gems to read how others honored them. Still, others of you may search to see what a certain stone can do for you. Do it! Read all about them, these special gems.

The folklore of gems is one of the most interesting passed down to us. You may even have a story of your own to share with your friend or mate about one of your favorite gems.

Read about the gems you would like to have. Look up the gemstones in your own collection. They may have energy influences so important to you that they could change your life.

The histories and legends reported in this chapter concerning each stone come from the many reference materials I have been collecting for years, story after story, from books, and from many noted persons, authors and sources. One of those sources that I would like to mention and give credit to is Reverend Michelle Lusson, a noted wellness counselor and diagnostician in northern Virginia. With her help in correcting some of my misinterpretations of gem properties, I hope that I have been able to categorize correctly the varied gem energies and their influence upon us.

Start with **A** for agates and continue to **Z** for zircon. You'll discover that agates can give to you additional support and strength, while zircons can help put you in the pink of life.

AGATES

Agates are the workhorse of the stone world; slow forming, steady and reliable. Agates are like strong medicine. When you need strength, protection, or support, there is surely one agate that does the job right. You can find these in a wide variety of patterns and colors. A family of variegated chalcedony or sard, they show colored bands, spots or markings. Some are striped, some are speckled, some are fossilized and some are solid. For identity purposes, agates are often named for the locales where they are found.

Agates were used for ornamentation and physical healing amulets, dating back to Babylon. Their medicinal uses continued throughout Ancient Greek and Egyptian civilizations, spreading through Africa and the Middle East, into Russia. Folklore mentions the use of agates as early as the 8th Century. They were often added to other stones to secure the actions of a stone. Rhodochrosite, a pink lace agate discovered by the Incas, was used with moonstone or garnet ornaments to increase the overall pink hue. The carnelian, an orange agate, was once one of the agates most prized by the Egyptians to represent nature organized into a building form or shape. Legends mention the power of agates to secure the wearer from danger and to protect children from falling. They were believed to endow their owners with strength, courage, security and even healing of fears. Early physicians used them for abdominal organ strengthening. Agates are found all over the world with some of the finest specimens occurring in the southwestern United States. Whatever your needs, security, strength, or support, the agates are there to serve you.

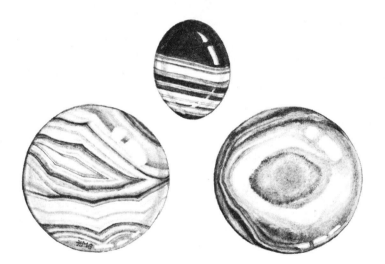

Agates

INDIAN AGATES

Folklore abounds about the Indian agates, particularly those with an eye. They were always used for protection against any type of evil influence or negativity. Major civilizations in the Middle East and Africa report over and over again the use of these agates to prevent injury and bodily harm. Since many early civilizations were primarily concerned with their physical survival, eye agates were often used as an offering to appease the Gods of the elements, to protect their harvests from drought, flooding or insect invasions.

You can use an eye Indian agate to help you with your survival.

MOSS AGATES

Moss agates are stones which appear to have growing plants inside. They come in many varieties, which include the green and red moss agate, the fern or plume agates, and the white and green tree agates. These agates were the miraculous healers of the tribal priests in the past, for they deemed them to have powers to interact with our human organic system. Over the centuries, moss agates were considered the most powerful of medicines to make warriors both strong and victorious over their enemies. They protected against poisonous reptiles, aided in cleaning out poisons, and stimulated the healing of wounds. These plant-like stones were believed to increase longevity and support the wearer's strength to ward off self-induced anger, bitterness, and other bad vibrations. A moss or fern agate will act as a cleanser for almost any cause. They can clear your personal energy system as well as your environment. Besides cleansing, the moss agate can be used as a body strengthener in times of stress. You can use a red moss agate as an aid to your physical exercise program when you give your body additional physical stress. A tree agate helps relieve tensions or fears, particularly when those fears are a concern with your health. Wear your moss agates for exercise as you would use a color for energy.

PLUME AGATES

This popular Southwestern agate, a form of moss agate, has a fiery red, grass-like plumage that shoots through the stone like a brilliant sunburst. Plume agates can encourage creative visualization, that is, to create an image of what you want, and then to achieve your goal. Its special property aids you to keep focused. For this reason, a plume agate can be a good job hunting stone to carry in your pocket.

DENDRITIC AGATES

Have you ever noticed an agate that looks like a firehouse dog, milky white with blue or brownish black stars? It reverses the night sky of dark blue with white stars. A dendrite or dendritic agate is one of the most powerful protective stones for travel, for it can prevent you from getting fatigued or having an accident when traveling down the highway. Put one in your suitcase or in your car. If you're a traveling salesperson, put one in your pocket or purse, especially when traveling by air.

BANDED AGATES

The banded agates have layers of agatized quartz, giving an appearance of bright bands or stripes. They too are the strong protectors, reinforcing your strength and providing protection if you are a very sensitive person. Wearing a banded agate is like taking extra Vitamin B. It is recommended if you are someone who needs extra courage or extra energy to face your stresses. For you who are drained by upsetting energies in your environment, it is an excellent stone. Banded agates have been reported to ease spastic discomfort from within, as well as from without. You might call them an antispasmodic soother stone as well as stress relieving. When you are under heavy stress, you often express yourself as being tied in knots and the bands of the agate can untie those holds. They can serve to keep out your tensions. This is a "call out the troops for protection" stone.

LACE AGATES

The fossilized lace agates have circular designs like many pebbles dropped into water. Lace agates can appear in almost any color from red, pink, white, yellow to blue. The most popular is the Mexican lace agate. Lace agates aid attitudes. They have been reported to even ease depression and despair. Their energy effect is circular and flowing. When you're feeling down and out, the lace agates will open up your door and encourage your flow. A Mexican lace agate, because of its usual deep red coloring, can bolster and strengthen your attitude. Another popular lace agate is blue lace, a wonderful calmer for your emotions and mind. You might consider it a blue detergent stone, like Cheer, to wash away your mental clutter. On the other hand, a white lace agate is sometimes called "happy lace." It can support optimism or elevate your thoughts. A pink lace agate can also add to your happiness by helping you to rescue your attitude.

Lace agates do not protect, they encourage and support. Lace agates show how gracefully a stone life form, through its very design and color, can have a wonderful stimulating effect on your attitude just by the transference of its flowing energy of design. Lace agates are most beautiful, so let them bring out your inner beauty.

BOTSWANA AGATES

Mined in Africa, the Botswana agate is one of the most popular banded agates for protection. Ancient Africans used them often in fertility rites, believing that they could strengthen their expressions of physical sexual energy.

Maybe you've experienced a physical loss or are lonely. Try this powerful banded agate with its lavender hue to ease your pain. A Botswana agate can also protect you if you are super sensitive, especially in crowds. It has strong bands, so let them wrap themselves around you.

An artist peer and friend of mine lost her husband suddenly due to a heart attack. This tragic loss created many changes in her life but, like so many of my wonderful associates, she was determined to continue her work as a painter. Her main problem was loneliness. I designed a necklace for her of Botswana agate beads, garnets and amethysts. The strand of bead gems had a lovely gray and lavender hue which unobtrusively coordinated with many of her outfits from navy blue to wine. She wore her necklace constantly. To her own amazement, her artistic works improved; she won many awards for outstanding paintings. In some way, this self-satisfaction was compensatory for some of her feelings of loneliness. She felt that the Botswana agates, in their own special manner, had aided her in adjusting to her new life and growth as an artist.

ALEXANDRITE

Alexandrite, a chrysoberyl, is a scarce and costly gemstone today. The quality of its color change determines, for the most part, its price and value.

The alexandrite is a transparent stone whose color varies with the light. From green to blue-green in the daylight it changes to mauve, violet or red in incandescent light. This magnificent property makes it a multi-purpose gem, a treat at any price. During the day, when it reflects blue-green, you might use an alexandrite to stimulate your happiness, good fortune, and success, but at night, when red, how about using it to become more sensual, warm and loving? Alexandrites can become an earth support to you who may not know how to play.

The stone has a history closely tied to Russia, being named for Czar Alexander I when it was discovered on his birthday. Since alexandrites are very rare and expensive, the synthetic stone of alexandrite is one of the few synthetic gems that can act as effectively as the real stone. They have the same light refracting qualities and properties.

You might consider the alexandrite a storehouse of pleasant surprises, particularly when the sun goes down.

AMAZONITE

Classified more as a feldspar mineral called microcline than a gemstone, amazonite deposits are located primarily in the South and North Americas. In gem and cabochon form, amazonite appears as a translucent, pearly, prismatic white, pink, or pale azure blue crystalline stone, with a surface luster resembling finely cracked or spider-webbed marble. Amazonite was once used as decorative material in building facades, yet now the material is sold by the pound to hobbyists for cabochoning and beads.

Because of having long been considered a mineral rather than an ancient gem there is not much folklore concerning amazonite, except for an important legend that tells us of its use as a "Hope Stone." Perhaps it was its very color of the spring sky that inspired faith and hope, or its strong potassium content that strengthened physical stamina. But, for whatever reason - faith, hope, or endurance - amazonite can offer to you additional strength in handling your day-to-day stresses.

AMBER

Amber is the solidified, fossilized resin of extinct conifer trees. It is highly valued for its inclusions of insects, leaves and organic debris trapped within the sap during formation.

In ancient times, amber was not only used for decoration in all forms of carvings, but early doctors prescribed grinding amber into powder and adding water to make a potion for the relief of stomach distresses. Mixed with honey, or oils, it was often prescribed as a salve for various physical pains and injuries. Worn on the body, it was reported to protect health as well as being especially favored as a symptomatic relief for headaches, toothaches, respiratory discomforts, infections and rheumatic pains. Ancient medicine men honored amber as an elixir to heal just about everything except love.

Eastern civilizations burned amber for its soothing effects and its disinfectant abilities, for they believed that amber filtered germs by sterilizing an area, especially during childbirth.

This honey colored stone radiates powerful amounts of heat and light, and possesses intense magnetic energy. In fact, it is probably the most magnetic stone that we have. That is why amber can be a most effective energy gem. Amber has a low thermal conductivity and feels warm to the touch. This adds to its attraction as a rubbing stone in order to bring out its soothing effects.

You might recognize amber as yellow, brown or an orange color, but it does occur in red or cherry orange. Central America and the Caribbean Islands are known for their honey colored amber, while in the Baltic, amber is found opaque and in colors of red or yellow. It is one of the softest gems to polish or facet, registering on the Mohs scale #2.5 to #3, and it will scratch so easily that attention must be paid to its setting. Rub your amber as well as wear it!

AMETHYST

Most of you recognize the beautiful North American amethyst, a crystalline purple quartz found in volcanic extruding rocks. A very popular stone among the Egyptian, Greek, Roman, English, and American civilizations, it has been given more honor than most other semiprecious stones. Its color, pale purple to violet, with flashes of wine, is strongly suggestive of its religious and spiritual uses in the past, as well as the present. Jewish priests wore it to symbolize spiritual power; it was the center stone of their identity breastplate. The Romans used it as a stone of physical power over the will of the people. Egyptians used the amethyst as a healing stone to ease fears and guilt and as a strong protector while traveling. When Egyptian ambassadors had to venture outside their major cities, they hung the amethyst around their necks for protection, for they believed it safeguarded them from personal treachery and surprise attacks. The Greeks named the stone "amethysts," meaning without drunkenness, and both the Greeks and the Romans used it constantly to protect themselves from excesses of overindulgence with food and drink. Goblets were inlaid with amethyst to prevent intoxication. The stone had such powerful healing effects upon the mind that it was often placed under pillows at bedtime to cure insomnia, to induce pleasant dreams, and for self-healing. For headaches, the stone was warmed and placed on the forehead or temples to reduce throbbing symptoms.

Considered a powerful psychic stone to safeguard against witchcraft and black magic, amethysts have been known to lose their color and turn pale when placed near an angry attacker. Yet, the major spiritual property of the amethyst was to aid second sight or to open up the spiritual or psychic center of the mind. Always identified as the stone of royalty and as the bishop's stone, it is still worn on the second finger of the right hand of a Catholic bishop, to symbolize ecclesiastical dignity.

Wear an amethyst if you want to get in touch with your intuition, your own feelings, or your own values. The stone has remarkable influences enhancing your mind, your intuition, and your insights concerning practical things. You can use it as an aid for meditation and to lift your spirits. When wearing an amethyst, you won't be tempted to overindulge, particularly in drinking, and when held in your left hand or worn around your neck, you can use it as an aid to get in touch with your inner self. If you are seeking greater intuition, keep an amethyst in your collection.

AQUAMARINE

Have you ever noticed a pale blue transparent crystal that becomes more brilliant in artificial light? Once considered a sacred stone, it is called aquamarine. The Romans were the first to call it by that name, which means "water of the sea," for it was used by Roman fishermen for protection on the water and to bring about a good catch. Even the Roman physicians used it as a prescription for overeating, believing the stone helped digestion of food and reduction of body fluid retention. Because it was considered such a purifier, the Roman craftsmen made goblets of aquamarine.

This gemstone of sailors is still believed to possess the calming, soothing, cleansing effect of the sea. You can use aquamarine to calm your nerves and, like water, to relax your body. It is an excellent gemstone for you to wear when traveling over water. When overexerted, why not slip into something cool and refreshing like your aquamarine?

AVENTURINE

Aventurine (also known as "Indian Jade") is either green, blue or red, a quartz-like rock made of tightly packed quartz which contains crystals of chrome-rich mica, giving the stone a metallic iridescence. Found in India and several South American countries, aventurine has been a popular rock to tumble for the past 50-100 years. The ancient Tibetans decorated their statues with aventurine, using it most often for the eyes of the statues, to symbolically increase visionary powers.

You might use aventurine as an opportunity stone to increase your perception. It can work as a gambler's stone for luck in games of chance. Try wearing it when you need a little something extra in your favor, or even to increase your opportunities. Put it in your pocket, take it to the race track or on your first date, and give yourself an aventurine chance.

AZURITE

Azurite, a dark blue gem, is found in the upper oxidized portions of copper deposits, and is often found mixed with malachite. It appears in a mixed color range from dark greenish blue to a blue black with sometimes the hardness of turquoise, or sometimes the hardness of agate.

Ancient Romans and Egyptians used the azurite for greater insight, for visionary powers, and particularly for hypnosis. Azurite, like the family of copper stones, can reduce personal stress and relax inner confusion.

You might use it to clear your thoughts, while at the same time to aid you in developing mental control over your emotions and reactions. Like amber, it is a rubbing stone that prefers to be touched to release its energies. So if you wear azurite, remember to rub it often to wipe the blues away.

BONE and IVORY

Bone and ivory have an ancient history as carving stones and as facial and neck decorative jewelry. Carved into every form, bone and ivory are often confused for they have similar properties and identities. The highly prized ivory netsukes were carved into animal and human forms, and worn suspended from the Buddhist Monk's girdle as prayer beads to represent higher human virtues. Bone and ivory prayer beads have more religious history than most other gemstones. They were not only used by Eastern religions for prayer beads of choice but by Western Christians as prayer beads of rosaries. They become more beautiful when rubbed because their sheen increases with human touch.

Ivory necklaces carved in India and China are the finest in the world. Yet, due to the diminishing supply of ivory tusks, many pieces of jewelry today are being carved from bone. The hardness is not exactly the same yet the work is as beautifully executed and can be prized for the artisan's skill. If you have antique ivory jewelry or ivory ornaments, you should value these pieces with pride since they are increasing in monetary value. Ivory will brown with age and rubbing. Do not clean, as the discoloration increases the sheen and finish.

You can rub ivory or bone and feel better; they are both soothing gifts from one animal to another.

Carved Ivory Eskimo Button

BLOODSTONE (HELIOTROPE)

Bloodstone is the most famous member of the jasper family. An opaque stone of intense dark green with blood red or orange oxide spots, it is considered a semiprecious stone, rather than a rock, as are most other jaspers. Legends surround the bloodstone more than any other jasper stone.

The earliest widely known legend of the Middle Ages states that the bloodstone was formed at the crucifixion of Jesus Christ when the blood of his wounds dropped on the dark green earth and turned to stone. From this legend comes the name bloodstone and the belief that the stone has exceptional wound healing powers. Yet bloodstones were known long before the time of Christ as heliotropes. Heliotrope means "sun turn." One Greek legend held that the heliotrope reflected the sun in the earth as blood red.

Many of the powers attributed to the bloodstone included the correcting of the mind and the giving of strength and courage. Its tremendous therapeutic powers reportedly cleared bloodshot eyes, relieved sunstroke and headaches, and most importantly, cured hemorrhage. As an amulet, it was used to prevent injury or disease.

Egyptian physician/priests used the bloodstone in healing potions. Ground, powdered and mixed with honey, it was believed to cure tumors and to stop hemorrhaging of all kinds. As an aid to circulation, the ancients dipped the stone in cold water and then placed it on the body.

Practically, bloodstone (heliotrope) can be a change or "turn-over" stone, as its name implies, for it is a powerful energy mover. Like an immense earth moving machine, the bloodstone can sweep away blocks, allowing you to move forward. Bloodstones as pendants or hip pocket stones can be used to support good circulation. The red specks in the bloodstone are a result of iron compounds, and iron is the basic mineral in your blood. Since stones can transfer their energies into your body, you can see the connection. According to the bloodstone's legendary history, it might be helpful to those of you who have had heart traumas due to stress or heart attack. Every one of you should have this royal-looking stone in your wardrobe to prevent blocks or traumas and to boost your energy flow. Professional healers might do well to have a bloodstone around them at work, as the bloodstone has always been considered "the healing stone."

I have a wonderful story to relate about a bloodstone's remarkable ability to remove blocks and what changes occurred.

A few years ago, an associate of mine, a female lobbyist in public relations, was going through a stressful time in business. The clients she represented were having a difficulty in communications with certain lawgivers concerning future outcomes of a community planning project. The clients were pushing for an immediate solution of the problem and the legislators had no intention of making an instant decision.

She found in my stone collection a beautiful large bloodstone, over half of the green jasper colored red with large iron oxide spots. After borrowing this multi-colored stone, she placed it in her purse, and off to work she went to try to solve the negotiation problem. Often during the day she reached into her purse to rub her jasper bloodstone while hoping the communications would go well. It was a yes or no decision to be made, but there were so many obstacles in the way. All of a sudden the tide swung for a positive decision and she was elated. She had done her job well.

The next morning with the same purse in her hand she came into the office. She reached in to pull out the helpful bloodstone and to her amazement and mine it was no longer the same stone. Its coloring had changed. The stone was still green, but now the red spots had changed to white without a trace of red left. The iron had removed itself in order to push away the blocks and the bloodstone's energy had done its work. I honored this bloodstone and kept it in my collection for a period of time and then returned it to the elements by tossing it away on the mesa one fair Saturday afternoon.

CARNELIAN

Carnelian, the most popular of the agates, has a varied history. It is a vitreous translucent stone of red-orange, dark to red brown, salmon, or sienna to rust, whose name comes from the Latin word, "flesh". In ancient Egypt it was thought to be the stone of form and design worn by master architects, to show their rank of builder. Because it's frequently found in the tombs of Egypt, carnelians are assumed to have been highly honored among the Egyptian people. Ancient warriors wore carnelians around their neck for courage and for physical power to conquer their enemies.

The alchemists of the Middle Ages used the carnelian as a boiling stone to activate the energy of other agates in order to transform energy into form according to the property of the particular agate. They considered it a metaphysical energizer to physical form.

Your carnelian can motivate you, and give you the energy to turn your ideas into form. For a directional aid, you can use it for job hunting. As a stone to balance your emotions, it can help your actions to become more personally satisfying. A carnelian can even restore your ambition that you might have lost and provide you with that additional energy to carry out those personal directives. Carnelian is the most powerful action stone for focusing, realization and self-actualization.

Since the color orange has a tendency to stimulate appetite, use your orange carnelian to stimulate your appetite for success, but watch your diet or you may increase your physical form.

A client of mine had been spending a great deal of time and money on books, courses, and tapes on positivity in order to enhance her sales career. She had recently changed her career from secretarial to sales, where the standard salesperson dressed in dark, sober clothes without jewelry, in order to follow an unpretentious sales image. Yet she liked warm sunny colors such as orange or rust, gold and yellow. She arrived in my office wanting to clear up her confusion about her personal image. Her colors were expressing manifestation, focus and achievement desires. I recommended carnelians, gold and topaz to accent a new wardrobe. This jewelry would help her project the energy that she desired.

Almost immediately she purchased pendants, beads and earrings of carnelians along with gold chains. Later these stones influenced a new color change in her entire wardrobe.

The first six months she doubled her production levels and by the end of the year she was chosen as Sales Executive of the Year for a large insurance sales company. During that time, several articles were written on her abilities to prospect and how her attitude and sunshine image closed the sale. Her co-workers, who at first were quite envious of her positive attitudes and her glamorous image, later followed by wearing more of their favorite gems.

Today, she is a successful, independent, financial planner who not only credits herself for her secured positive image, but who also gives honor and acknowledgment to her favorite gemstone, a carnelian.

CAT'S EYE/TIGER'S EYE

For these eye stones, we will group together all the animal eyes, such as cat's, tiger's and falcon's. The star chrysoberyls are often considered the finest of the cat's eye stones, for they are the most valued chrysoberyls. They are honey brown in color with a shadow effect when light strikes them obliquely. In light, their side away from the source of light appears rich brown, while the other side facing the light becomes yellowish white. This is called a "milk and honey" effect and characterizes the perfect cat's eye gemstone, so called because it resembles the narrow iris in the eye of the cat.

Of the other mineral "eye" stone formations, crocidolite is the other major cat's eye gemstone. Crocidolite is a fine grained quartz, zonally designed with a silky texture. When cut as a cabochon, the translucent stripes have the appearance of a glowing eye. Among this grouping we find the popular brown tiger's eye and the blue falcon's eye. Yet of the eye stones the cat's eye has been considered the most powerful in folklore tales.

The eye stones were often feared by the ancients because the person who wore them supposedly could see everything, even behind closed doors. The cat's eye was a popular good luck stone and was used often as an amulet. When you're afraid of making an incorrect decision, you might try one to help you think clearly before you act. It will help you to see what you are getting into before you get into it. On the other hand if you are too impulsive, put your cat's eye on your finger to look straight ahead.

The falcon's eye, crocidolite, is usually gray blue and is the most authoritative or bossy of the eye stones. You can use it to increase self-understanding, or when your life gets out of control. The falcon's eye should help to put you back in your own driver's seat.

Tiger's eyes have the most popular appeal and price of the eye stones. This brown eye gem can support your insight and perception. Historically, the Egyptians used the tiger's eye as the eyes in their god-image statues to express divine vision. On your finger, use the tiger's eye for decision making and creative stimulation. If you're entering a new creative profession, tiger's eye should be one of the first tools of your new trade.

Carry eye stones for clear thinking, accurate judgment, for protection and for good luck. Put your eyes on and see clearly.

CHALCEDONY

Chalcedony is the general name given to translucent quartz agates which have speckles, plumes or striations. In the history of the agates, chalcedony and sard have gone hand in hand with their energy properties, but chalcedony will usually contain patterns of humus or plant debris calcified within, giving this agate additional earth elemental energy properties.

One of the most popular of the chalcedonies is the luna agate. The name must have been given because of its resemblance to the universe. The stone appears as clear, almost transparent, containing snowpuffs, or snowflakes of white agatized materials. A luna agate is a wonderful agate to aid in linking your mind with your feelings. It might even help you to clear away the cobwebs of your past in order to make your future clear and beautiful.

Another popular chalcedony is the Montana agate which resembles the luna agate, but contains black agatized materials forming pictures and images. The luna agate portrays the universe and the Montana agate, our world in three dimensions. Both the luna and the Montana agates' energy properties are similar for they can aid you to be more content with yourself by linking your thoughts with your feelings. These are two more agates for your gem or rock box.

My husband and I were collecting rocks, particularly agates, from north of Bernalillo, New Mexico, when I came across a wonderful area for luna agates; the milk white puffs in the honey-stained agatized quartz were magnificent. They were truly a rock hound's perfect specimen of luna agates.

My mother-in-law's 75th birthday was on the horizon and I decided to cut a large cabochon from these newly collected agate specimens for a pendant for her gift. I wanted to give her a luna agate for I knew that she was having some difficulty releasing some traumas of the past. I did not mention to her the energy legends of these agates, only informed her that the stone had come from the nearby countryside. I wanted to see for myself if the famed chalcedony agate folklore had any validity in affecting human response.

She enjoyed the lovely milky white design of the luna agate stone in the pendant and wore it constantly. Slowly but surely, her conversations began to change and less and less she talked about some of her past traumatic experiences. Whether she felt that my husband and I had heard all the stories too many times before or whether the luna agate was taking effect, we don't really know. But what we do know is that there was a positive outcome, and just maybe it was due to a stone!

CHRYSOCOLLA

Chrysocolla is a copper stone, light green to deep blue, found in most copper mines and formed similarly to turquoise; that is, in the oxidized zones of copper deposits. Its luster and hardness depend upon its quartz content. Sometimes its hardness is like that of the agate, or it sometimes appears like the turquoise.

The history of chrysocolla coincides with the history of other green stones, for many of the legends originate in the Far East. Often it was called green turquoise and not considered a stone in its own right. Yet, when cited as a semiprecious gemstone of its own right it was favored as a stone for prosperity, luck, and business astuteness. The power of chrysocolla, like a balance scale, can act to stimulate the mind and relax the emotions at the same time. It reacts upon your analytical and intuitive abilities. Together its energy influence alleviates emotional confusion while expanding your mind to new awareness and understanding. As a copper mineral gem, chrysocolla opens bottled emotions that can block the mind from thinking clearly. Chrysocolla is a good choice for a stone when you have difficulty expressing your feelings. If you work in the computer design industry, programming or analyzing, a chrysocolla can help keep you from short-circuiting like one of your machines. For you designers and inventors, a chrysocolla will help combine your creative ideas with new practical applications.

Keep a chrysocolla in your work space, for its balancing effect can improve the results of your work.

CORAL

Coral, an organic gem, is a gift from the sea. It is the plant-like skeleton of minute marine animals who lived in the ocean. Varied in color, coral is pale to deep red, all shades of pink and orange, white and even sometimes black. Its favor as a healing gem dates back to the empires of Egypt, of Rome and Greece. Physical safety was often guaranteed for the traveler who wore coral. Ancients believed that coral could balance the body, relax the emotions and mind, and promote a strong and stable personality.

Red coral was credited with the power to destroy bad energy vibrations. The Romans used it to protect and heal their children, many times hanging it around their necks to protect against respiratory diseases, or even rubbing it into their gums to alleviate teething pains. When wore around the neck, legend states, the coral would turn pale when its wearer became sick, regaining its color only when health returned. Red coral was worn also by newly married couples as a protection against sterility. Deep orange coral was worn to release pent-up energies. It has been said that if the coral broke when wearing it, it was to be thrown away and never worn again for it had given up its life energy for protection.

Red coral is an excellent choice for a first gemstone to give small children, as it can strengthen and support their growth. Besides, children love its red color!

Orange coral can be good for those of you who lack self-satisfaction. White or pink coral can be worn as organizing boosters for they can help you get your act together. All corals will help support your physical energy and relax your tensions after a long, hard day. You can even use some coral to restore your voice after using it all day. Take heed, teachers and talkers.

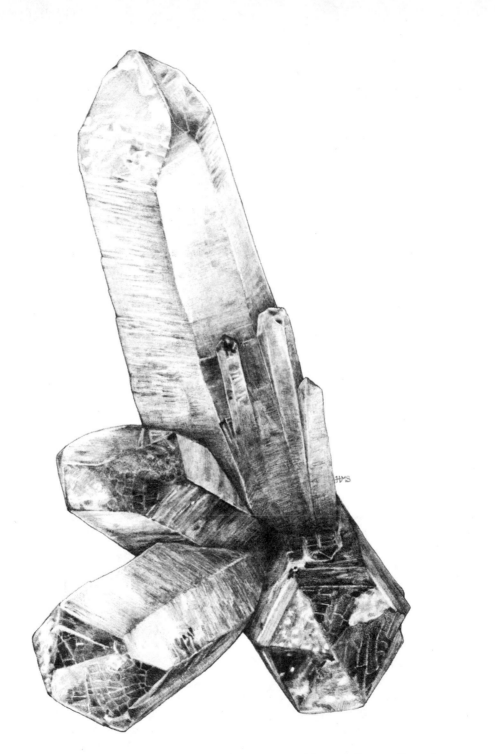

Natural Quartz Crystal

CRYSTAL

Crystals, crystals everywhere making rainbow fractures of light. The quartz crystal is the most common mineral in the world, a combination of silicon and oxygen, but rock crystal is the clearest form of quartz crystal. Through the course of history, these spikes of quartz have often been considered a perfect jewel. Crystal as a gemstone has been held in high esteem for centuries as its owners have noted its elevating properties of energy as well as its practical use as an energy conductor. Rock crystal is sometimes credited with having its own inner light, for when rubbed, the excitation of electrons produces rainbow flashes within its fractures.

The history of the crystal goes back to ancient civilizations, even that of Atlantis, where the sun's power was believed to be harnessed through a crystal as a source of solar energy refraction. It is written in gem folklore that the crystal contained a universe unto itself. The rock or spike crystal gets its name from the Greek word, *krystallos,* meaning "ice," because the Greeks thought the crystal was water frozen forever hard into ice by the gods. Sir Isaac Newton discovered the color spectrum by refracting sunlight through a natural crystal. Reflecting the rainbow on his wall allowed him to measure the different lengths of the rays of our visible light spectrum. Crystals are still associated with prisms, cut glass and other visual instruments for refracting light and capturing the rainbow. This enhances the theories of the ancients who claimed the sun and the light universe were housed within a perfect crystal.

Look at your crystal. Crystals absorb light, refract light, and share light. They can be cut or faceted like a diamond. When we use it, the crystal can become an all-around self-energy generator and light balancer. Those of you who influence people should have crystal in your environment to help you generate energy. A crystal can function as your personal source. Don't mistake silicon or sand crystals for rock crystals, for they are man-made glass crystals. Although beautiful, they are not as effective as gem energy healers as the natural crystals. For crystal beauty, the aurora crystals from Vienna are the finest in the world and cannot compare with other man-made crystals.

Your crystals can offer you an indoor sun world for warmth, strength and vitality. Some of you may even prefer a crystal ball, for legends claim they can encourage inner sight. If you meditate, daydream or just gaze into a crystal, what a high you can get; your mind perceives the light that is reflected and transformed by the energy of the universe.

DIAMOND

For those of you who are into diamonds, you should know that a diamond is considered by most of the world to be the king of gems. It has amazing properties of hardness, superior to any other gemstone, and a brilliance which is unique. Diamonds are crystals of pure carbon, the element that is the foundation of life, and are formed under conditions of intense heat and pressure. If the energy of a diamond could be released, the force of the resulting explosion would be unimaginable.

Because of its exceptional brilliance, the diamond has a considerable history. It was worn by the aristocratic families to ward off the plague that hit Europe during the Middle Ages. When the ships brought the plague into the harbors, the poor people who lived near the ports were the first to die. Therefore, the wealthy thought that if they wore diamonds, they would be immune to the Black Death. Actually, this remedy was ineffective since diamonds do not ward off anything. In fact, they absorb just about everything.

Another time in history, diamonds were used as a poison by the upper classes. The stone was ground into a powder and put into an enemy's food or drink. The deaths of many prominent people have been attributed to this method of diamond poisoning. There are many legends that diamonds were supposed to have mystical powers to ward off any dangers because of their brilliance, and to protect their wearers from bad dreams, demons and nightmares like a continual shining light.

Below the earth's crust diamonds are formed at great depths, under intense heat and pressure, then rising up from the earth's mantle to the earth's surface. The resultant pure crystalline form has no life of its own, giving the diamond the lone property to absorb all energies.

The Hope Diamond

When you hold a diamond, it can feel cold to your touch. This is because of its high thermal conductivity, whereupon it can suck into itself the warmth of your body. It possesses a high psychic energy as well and can easily magnetize into its radiant fields thoughts and actions. Due to this great absorption power, you should clean your diamonds often to rid them of any negative energies they might have taken in. Soak your diamond for at least one hour in an ionic solution of a teaspoon of salt and a teaspoon of baking soda, dissolved in eight ounces of water. Rinse well. Your diamond will feel better and shine brighter.

Symbolically, diamonds have been associated with love, innocence and security of love. Their great brilliance is their popular power. In Twentieth Century America, the diamond is traditionally a love-bearing gift. The engagement ring, the wedding ring and other jewelry symbolize the gift of persons in love. Many of you also feel that diamonds offer security and success, for diamonds are associated with wealth, power and prestige, because of their monetary value alone. But are they really? Are they really a girl's best friend?

EMERALD

The emerald, a deep green precious gem, is the most famous of the beryl family. Named from the Persian word for green, the emerald has always been surrounded by deep mystery. The Greeks dedicated this stone to the Goddess Venus, believing that it ensured security in love. Orientals believed that this green gem strengthened memory, increased intelligence, and gave those who wore it the power to foretell future events. The association of the emerald with sight and the eyes has been reported by many civilizations. It was once thought that emeralds even had the power to cure diseases of the eyes. Always considered a great insightful prophecy stone, the emerald, according to legend, would hurl itself from its mounting in order to forewarn of pending danger of illness. The distinctive emerald green color is due to the presence of chromium in the beryl, although some believed that the emerald also contains chlorophyll, which would account for the ancient use of the stone as an antiseptic.

The Incas worshipped the emerald, while on the other side of the world the Jewish high priest selected it as one of his breastplate gems, in the certainty that it represented universal attainment. During the Middle Ages the emerald was thought to protect a woman's chastity and to preserve the love and esteem of her husband, similar to the Greeks' version of the emerald securing love.

The emerald has often been considered the true symbolic gem of hope and faith. It has, as well, an important folklore background as a gem link with the spiritual parts of self, often considered the symbol of psychic power and immortality.

The light energy of an emerald can aid you in strengthening your memory, enhancing your speech, and can act as a natural tranquilizer when you are worried or your mind is troubled. Long considered a gemstone of universal sight, your emerald has the power to strengthen your perception and insight while stimulating self-truth and love from others.

There are many persons today who prefer emeralds over diamonds, symbolically representing security of love. I am one of those people who loves emeralds. In fact, I have an emerald set in my wedding band, not for the constancy of love alone that it brings to me, but because I believe emeralds stimulate universal insight and open-mindedness. The emerald is a great gemstone for worriers to clear their minds, as well as a stone for promoting creativity and fertile ideas. My emerald, although quite small, is my constant companion to support my creative mind and to help me see clearly and objectively the world around me. So if you desire to see your full creative potential, see with an emerald!

GARNET

Varying in size and color according to the part of the world in which they are found, the garnet family has its own special identity. You can recognize garnets as ruby red pyropes; brown or orange almadines; glossularites which are cinnamon colored; and andradites, green in color - to mention a few of the family members. These varied colored garnets are used widely in industrial markets, from watch gears and scientific instruments to sandpaper and abrasives of many kinds.

The name garnet came from the Latin word, "granatus" meaning "like seeds," as they are found seeded in many rocks. Yet some garnets have been as large as melons; Pliny reported that the Indian carbuncle garnet was large enough to be carved into a water jar.

Not only as jewelry and ornamental gems, garnets have a potent and vast folklore. They were once noted for their powerful protective energies. They were thought to have medicinal abilities to reduce body toxins and to heal emotional problems. Some ancient Asiatic tribes used red garnets as bullets for sling bows because they pierced their victims quickly, and could not be seen well in the body when they mingled with the blood. At other times, the stones were placed in wounds to help heal by encouraging the clotting of the blood. As an amulet they were worn on the body for strong protection against poisons. Placed under a sufferer's pillow, garnets were thought to alleviate bad dreams while other medicine men used them to provide a curative for mental depression. Over and over again, legends mention garnets for their strong curative powers.

Garnets can act as strong help to balance your energy system and stimulate your desires and uplift your attitude. As a balancer stone, a garnet can prevent fears of insecurity and even money losses. Garnets are lucky stones: lucky for love, lucky for success and lucky for goals. You can use your garnets to increase your positivity and popularity, for everyone likes a positive, happy person. And, of course, this can enhance your personal self-esteem. As an energy stone, a garnet can encourage success in business and in business relationships, even stimulating your fellow workers' desires to work better with you. They make wonderful executive gems, especially for women. But if your garnets happen to absorb too many of your insecurities and fears, they can become pitted or dull, even lost. You have drawn from them their red light of positivity and they have no life left with which to shine. The ancient Hebrews named the garnet "barak", meaning lightening, and one legend states that Noah in the Ark suspended a garnet to diffuse light for energy refracted earlier from the sun. So to shine your red light of positivity and in order to be successful, wear a garnet.

GEODES

These gem rocks are often called "thunder eggs" and are found as stone balls with a crystal, topaz, or amethyst center. Geodes sometimes have bands of jasper or agate surrounding their crystalline centers. Tiny or immense, they are found in all colors, as stones of great beauty. When sliced open, they reveal an unparalleled crystal universe within. The ones we prize the most are the geodes that contain amethyst.

Geodes are usually found in deposits where two massive land forms have come together. In formation, water between two rock bodies was unable to be released during the movement of the rocks. Eventually, a formed thunder egg was spit out and usually found rolling down the side of a mountain, like a rolling marble. Friction or rubbing created the shape of the stone ball geode similar to the way a mollusk forms a pearl. The legends of thunder eggs are like that of the onyx, a gift of the gods. Because of their supposed divine origin, a creation of the god of the elements, Thunder, geodes many times were used for prophecy readings by ancient tribes. These wonder stones are found abundantly in Mexico and in the southwestern United States. More often found in the Western Hemisphere, they have rarely been noted in the folklore of the Eastern world.

Geodes can be supportive for those of you who want to assert your independence. Like a friend, they can aid by stimulating independent thinking and freedom of spirit. Due to their crystalline nature, geodes also are energy generators and can stimulate good working habits. When you carry a small geode you are holding your world as you see it, and they can remind you of what image you want your world to be.

Be a free spirit, wear your tiny geode close to your heart and create an image of yourself in charge of your entire universe. Put your thunder egg on your desk and make your universe productive.

JADE

The gemstone jade comes in many colors, white, cream, black, pink and the most common and familiar, green. Far back in recorded history the Chinese associated green jade with occult wisdom, and jade is still the most popular stone used in China today for jewelry and carvings. Besides the ability to assure a long life and a peaceful death, the ancients attributed extensive healing powers to the jade.

Since jade was a stone to help inspire the mind to make a quick and precise decision, the ancient trader would often hold this gem in the palm of his right hand while he engaged in business transactions. The Greeks counted on the soothing and healing color of the stone for more direct physical applications, most particularly for ailments of the eyes. A piece of jade might have been placed directly on the eyelids or used in a cleansing eye solution. Still at other times, jade was ground into powder and used as an antidote for snake and rodent bites, and as a calming elixir for stomach ailments.

Jade amulets are rather common findings among the tombs and burial chambers of Egypt. Perhaps the Egyptians believed that these cool stones would peacefully guide and soothe the soul departing to the hereafter. Many of the Oriental figurines were carved in jade to represent not only divine objects of devotion, such as the Buddha, but also to honor the green stone itself. Sculptors would lovingly carve the jade stone to produce a figure arising out of the jade's own particular stone formation.

At least one legend from the stone's past overwhelms our current association of love with diamonds. A carved jade butterfly was the most powerful symbol of a successful romance. A smitten maiden gave such a stone to her lover to bind their engagement. You might try wearing a jade butterfly to stimulate love for yourself and to tie up your commitments.

Carry a piece of jade for getting things to work for you practically. If you want to be more pragmatic, you might place a jade object on your desk. Try to find a jade scarab to symbolically represent for you a long and prosperous life, one of luck and one of love. A piece of green jade can work also as a philosopher's stone to stimulate your wisdom and desired goals. Rub your jade for just pure sensual pleasure as you would rub a beautiful sculpture. Feel the stone and think cool, as jade.

JASPER

One of the most popular solid, opaque gemstones, with a hardness similar to that of agate, is jasper. It is found in red, rose, brown, yellow and even variegated greens. The Bible speaks often of red jasper. In Revelations, John beheld God's heavenly throne and stated, "The One seated is in appearance like a jasper stone."

The history of the jasper is intertwined with that of the agate and the bloodstone, and at times it becomes difficult to separate them historically. Yet jaspers are traceable to all ancient peoples and civilizations. Imperial jasper was an identity gemstone of one of the tribes of Israel. American Indians used jasper as a rubbing stone and certain tribes called it "the rain bringer." They divined the earth's energies for water with red jasper, possibly because it increased the searcher's sensitivity to the earth. For the Indians, jasper was known as a powerful amulet to protect against any unseen hazards of the night.

A strong, solid, securing stone, jasper is a stability stone. You might use jasper to reduce your insecurities, fears and guilt. This historical stone might also protect you from becoming over-emotionally involved with persons or things that are not good for you. The energy of the red jasper can influence the regulation of the metabolic energies of your body, while promoting more physical stamina. Brown jasper, a basic security stone, can influence your secu-

Picture Jasper

rity and stability. Green jasper has an effect upon your own well-being as it prevents you from being threatened by others. Rose jasper is a soothing emotional securer.

All jaspers have strengthening energy effects upon your emotional nature by easing emotional stresses. Relax, be secure, and wear the rainbow jaspers.

JET

For those of you who like black stones, jet is an interesting choice. It is a shiny black compressed coal, or lignite. Since Roman times, it has been one of the most popular of black gems. Jet has been called black amber and was honored for its mystical protective uses. During the Middle Ages, Italian craftsmen carved figurines of beetles from jet to use for amulets to ward off evil influences, a practice still around today. For their color alone, many black stones were carved as protective amulets with Roman travelers using black jet as a safeguard charm on a long and hazardous journey. Most commonly, jet was used, similar to amber and coal, as a filtering agent and was burned like incense.

When worn as a necklace, jet was associated with being a direct link of the body with the spirit soul. If you like to wear it, you should always take personal care in guarding it. Jet should never be exchanged from one person to another. You should consider it a one-person stone. You can also use it as your personal protection stone for safety while traveling. Because of its softness, it is easy to carve and a good stone for inlay gem jewelry. In settings, it is commonly placed alongside shell in order to enhance its color and protective qualities. Jet will take a good polish and can be faceted to add sparkle.

When you wear jet you can feel secure that people will have difficulty intruding on your space that day.

LAPIS LAZULI

Lapis lazuli is a deep magnificent royal blue stone containing traces of pyrite, calcite, or gold. Precious lapis lazuli has just a sprinkling of pyrite, for in gem quality solid blue is preferable. It is a very durable stone and does not show wear easily. It is believed that the original organic ultramarine pigment used in early paintings and cosmetics was obtained from powdered lapis. As a gem today, lapis is becoming more rare for its major source of supply is the Middle East and our supply has now become somewhat restricted. This opaque gemstone is one of the oldest spiritual stones known, for it was used mainly by priests and royalty in ancient Egypt. Many believe that the Biblical sapphire was actually lapis lazuli. Through the ages, lapis has been associated with power, wisdom, love, and most frequently as a stimulator for psychic abilities.

For the Egyptians, lapis lazuli was the most valued of gems. In fact, it was so precious to the ancient world that it was valued on a level equal to gold. Pieces of it were inscribed in the *Book of the Dead*, so as to guide the passage of the soul into its afterlife. The Pharaoh himself wore a lapis lazuli, carved in the likeness of an eye ornamented with gold, to constitute an amulet of the greatest power. The lapis represented universal truth. The papyrus texts reported that the lapis lazuli symbolized the might of the gods always present in Egypt. Ancient priest healers used the lapis as an energy stone to strengthen the mind and prepare the body for spiritual awareness.

You can wear a lapis to aid you to stimulate your inner vision, to give you enhanced wisdom, insight and good judgment. The lapis can act as a powerful think-tank stone. But you should not set lapis in jewelry with other stones whose energies can cancel out each other's desired effects, like lapis lazuli and turquoise. It is also not one of the best gems for your ears.

Yet the color of the lapis makes this stone an easy fit into almost any wardrobe. It will coordinate well with most of your fashion colors. Since it stimulates wisdom and good judgment in the practical world, lapis makes an excellent executive stone. Carry it in your pocket or wear it on your finger to show whomever, that this beautiful blue gem, lapis lazuli, can strengthen your intelligence and wisdom.

MALACHITE

Have you ever noticed a gemstone bright as Irish green? It probably is a malachite, a rich green opaque stone with lighter green eye-shaped forms or bands on its surface design. Composed of copper ore and occurring in the oxidized portions of ore mines, this stone is soft and sensitive, similar to the blue turquoise.

Historically, malachites were believed to enhance great visionary powers. Not only as potent stones of protection, they were also thought to stimulate just about every type of personal power. The malachite "eye stones" were used as third eyes to ward off any negative vibrations or happenings from outside self. Their most powerful association remaining today is their unique ability to warn their owners of approaching danger by breaking into two pieces.

The ancient Egyptians ground the malachite stone into a fine powder and used it as the first cosmetic eye shadow. This green eye adornment not only made a brilliant eye shadow, but was reported to stimulate clear vision and insight. The Egyptian physicians employed malachite in the treatment of circulatory diseases, because they believed the stone had curative properties for blood problems. The gemstone was often worn by children as a talisman, protecting them from bad dreams while giving to them a greater sense of emotional security.

You can use a green malachite to promote your inner peace and hope. It will aid in your business world success through its practical expedient of warding off undesirable business associations. Also it is another powerful copper gemstone source and you might utilize a malachite for the balancing effects of this mineral. Protection and inner security, the major actions of malachite, go hand in hand. Green, you're in luck and successful; broken, take heed!

MOONSTONE

Soft, watery-like, with a beautiful rolling pearly sheen, your gem is a moonstone. A variety of feldspar, moonstones are found in various delicate colors of the rainbow, such as pink, blue, green, and a lustrous white.

Since early times, this stone has been associated with moon magic. Logically, then, the ancients believed that the full moon increased their powers. Moonstones were named the traveler's stones because of the protection they afforded to many a night traveler, especially upon the water when the moon was shining. As a gem, the moonstone signified hope to ancient man and because of this uplifting quality it was popularly worn as a talisman or amulet to enhance the personality.

Another power of the moonstone was to promote love, for it was believed to be able to reunite loved ones who had parted in anger. The Romans even believed their beloved and honored moonstone enclosed the image of Diana, the moon goddess, who could endow love, wealth, victory and wisdom upon the fortunate possessor. Other legends bestowed the gifts of prophecy and second sight upon this stone, for many claimed that a moonstone could clear the mind, allowing its wearer to reach wise decisions and keep mind and heart in touch with one another.

A moonstone is a wonderfully sensitive stone. Consider it a lucky love stone, for it just might act that way when you are looking for love. When you are feeling emotionally overextended, try your moonstone for self-equalization. In the past, moonstones have been known to lose their silvery luster when their owners continued to hold within themselves a lot of anger. If your moonstone has changed its quality of shine, you might take a look at yourself to see what was going on in your world at that time. Your moonstone will become your aid in self-analysis. Don't be afraid to open up your love and let your moonstone guide you.

Moonstones can open your heart to nurturing qualities as well as to help you to accept experiences of love. At the same time, a moonstone will always protect your sensitive nature. What a beautiful, joyous, light stone. All of us should have at least one in our jewelry box.

An executive friend of mine was having difficulty in accepting his own sensitivities or feelings. For too long, he had attempted to maintain an image of self-control and self-management until he was losing contact with the needs of the persons who worked with him. In fact, it had even come to the point in his working social relationships that he was feeling left out and not included among his professional family. He did not exactly know how to cope with creating a new image of his loving qualities, for he really did care about his fellow persons.

I suggested that he might try carrying a moonstone in his hip pocket and rub it occasionally, asking it to aid him with its love magic. He took my advice and put a little moonstone in his left pocket.

The first day he carried it, nothing happened. But on the second day a business friend called him asking about a lunch together to talk about some personal problems. That same day, his secretary asked for some time off to go to the dentist and his wife called asking him to loan his company car to one of his children for the afternoon. Normally, he would have said no to all three requests; he really didn't want to be bothered with other people's problems. He needed his secretary that afternoon and normally he would have let his son make other arrangements for transportation. But on this particular day, he thought about the moonstone in his pocket and said yes to all. As a result, his friend brought him a new contract worth thousands of dollars for listening to some seemingly unimportant problems; his secretary returned to his office with flowers in order to thank him; and his wife, that evening, planned a fancy private dinner for him at home to thank him in a very personal way. His moonstone had begun to work. He felt appreciated.

OBSIDIAN

Obsidian is a volcanic glass, a transparent rock that appears in black, gray, or brown with bands, or white snowflakes. It is usually found in areas of present or former volcanic activity and is formed similar to a diamond. One of the favorite carving rocks for spearheads, it has been discovered in most areas of the world. Black obsidian figurines have also been found all over Central and South America carved in amulets and lucky charms. Small, sand-smoothed and -shaped pebbles of obsidian are called "Apache Tears," for legend states that the earth cried when an Apache warrior was killed in battle. Black obsidian with white dots contained within is commonly called snowflake obsidian and is a favorite cabochon stone of rock hounds for its transparent patterns.

Like jet, you should not exchange your obsidian with another person. It is a protection stone and will help to prevent emotional draining from others. Obsidian can also give you additional support when stressed from outside pressures. Obsidian stones help protect the soft-hearted and gentle people of the world from being misused. Its very color, black, acts like a screen to keep out the unwanted. Occasionally one will find obsidian in a spectrum color like dark blue and its very color can offer even greater protection, like a favorite navy blue suit. So if you ever feel overly troubled because of outside interferences, put your obsidian to work as your protective energy glass.

ONYX

Onyx can be another black stone or a variegated banded black and white chalcedony. Mexican onyx, a particular form of onyx, is a translucent veined quartz with white and subtle earth-color bands. Easily carved and dyed, it is used for just about everything ornamental from statues to chess pieces. The ancient Egyptians believed the onyx, when worn around the neck, could cool the ardors of love and provoke discord even to the point of separating lovers.

Although this stone has the energy effect of producing negative results, you may use it successfully and positively for release. For example, you could use it to end a bothersome relationship. On the other hand, too much onyx on your own body can create discordance within yourself, for it may dam up the flow of your natural energy. But dyed onyx won't do this, for its energy cells have been sealed in the dyeing. Wear your onyx for self-protection or place a carved figurine on your desk to keep away bothersome entanglements.

OPAL

Opals integrate the many faces of Eve. Some are milky, some are on fire, some are jelly, but all have the magic rainbow within. Opals are reported to be the oldest gemstones created from water and crystalline rock formations. Their market value depends upon the size of the stone, the color and pattern displayed, and most importantly, the amount of fire within. Precious black opals are the rarest. Opal deposits have often been discovered where gold occurs, and although a water-formed stone, opals can be brittle and crack spontaneously when not immersed in water. The opal is a mysterious gem, as each one appears different in its delicate beauty. Like an Eve, the more rainbow images an opal expresses, the more it has been prized by its owner.

Opals have always been one of the most popular and esteemed gems. In folklore, Octavius Caesar wished to sell one third of his vast Roman kingdom for a single opal. During the Crusades, the ladies gave their crusaders an opal to bring them good fortune in battle. The Egyptians and Babylonians honored the fire opal because they believed it to be a most powerful light and water healing gem. Opals were often placed on the navel of an expectant mother to provide an easier childbirth. Many cultures believed that the opal could open one's mind to visions, for the Greek astrologers and mediums constantly used them in prophecy and divination. In the Middle Ages, an amulet of opal alone or one that contained opals mixed with the other gems protected its wearer against increasing faulty vision, while strengthening the mind and memory.

Yet, through the ages, many disappointing legends sprung up about the opal. They were given a bad reputation in a novel written by Sir Walter Scott in which an opal played a malevolent part. Much negativity surrounded the opal because of the ease with which the stone cracked, and when given as a lucky or love stone, the splitting was usually taken as a sign of bad luck.

Opals have been known to absorb, carry and pass enormous amounts of energy. Their ability to absorb energy is comparable only to their ability to absorb water. The opal absorbs energy like the diamond, and transforms that energy and expresses it like a crystal.

However, most legends caution that all persons cannot and should not wear an opal. This may be because of the high internal energy of the opal stone. If you are not able to direct or even deal with powerfully focused energy, don't wear the opal; it can increase the magnitude of your thoughts and actions.

Because of their delicacy, you should separate your opals from the other gems in your jewelry box. The best way to keep them is to wrap them securely in a piece of cotton or place them in a small container of water. For continual care, a good way to water your opals is to put them on your fingers and run your hands under water (not hot water). Soap should not injure your opals, as they usually absorb only water. If stored uncut, opals can lose their rainbow fire and crack, unless they are stored in water.

In the most popular legend of all folklore concerning the opal, it is called the Cupid Stone, a stone of love and romance and a stone to grant wishes and personal happiness. Put your opal in your hand and give it a wish; it may favor your desire, especially if it is one for love. Its power may surprise you and bring you a unique love. The opal is truly the "Queen of Gems," the Eve of the Gods, a stone of hopes, positive actions, and achievements. You can make it one of your stones of love.

PEARL

Your pearl is a wondrous and mysterious creation. Pearls appear in white, blue, cream, rose, exotic grays and blacks. Their high lustrous sheen in diffused light is unequalled. A pearl is an organic gem, a mass of nacre secreted by various mollusks, particularly the oyster. Yet fresh water pearls are from river mussels, and cultured pearls, the perfectly rounded pearls, are from mollusks that have been commercially seeded with an irritant to produce a flawless pearl.

In all legends and folklore, pearls have been associated with femininity. Perhaps it was their unflawed beauty, their cool luster, their exquisite simple shapes, or their delicate toughness, but pearls have always been for the ladies. One legend acclaims the pearl's power to relax the mind to free up one's energy for more balanced love relationships. The Hindus believed the pearl, the mother gem of the sea, represented the moon's influence upon the earth, thereby protecting the earth from catastrophic weather.

Pearls can stimulate your femininity and help you with self-acceptance. Give a pearl to a child to help him or her grow in beauty, especially a little girl. Pearls are extremely sensitive and because of their energy sensitivity, they can be used up or lose their light luster. Your emotions can absorb their energy and make their life expectancy variable. If you're not paying enough attention to a healthy diet while you are constantly wearing your pearls, you can drain the life out of your pearls. Also, do not immerse your pearls in soaps or detergents. They respond negatively to these products and soap damages their luster.

Wear your pearls for beauty and see yourself as a pearl of great price.

I have a personal story concerning a small pearl ring that verifies the sensitivity of pearls and the ability to drain energy from your pearls.

I had inherited from my grandmother an exquisite small pink pearl three-pronged ring which instantly became one of my favorite rings to wear. As a young artist I was furthering my studies under private tutorship from a famous Italian painter who was very strict on techniques of painting and style. My master professor disciplined my work severely in order to improve my style of painting. It is necessary to say that this was not an ego-boosting period of my life and I suffered emotionally, as artists tend to do, to improve my work to please myself and my teacher. For months, my ring took the brunt of my exasperation. First, one of my pearls popped out of its setting, leaving only two where three had so proudly stood. I replaced the pearl after great difficulty in duplicating the exact color. Next, the second pearl lost its luster. If you've ever seen a dead pearl, as I had in my ring, it has no color at all. I replaced this pearl too. Finally, I decided to stop wearing my little ring constantly and returned it to my jewel box to await other days. My apprenticeship continued with my professor, yet his severity of teaching continued to make me feel miserable concerning my art career. Was there any hope for me to proceed? Since I loved my little pearl ring, I sought its company and occasionally put it on to comfort me. One morning when dressing, I opened my jewel box to gaze at my little ring, and to my sadness, all three pearls were lifeless. They could not give any more to boost my low self-esteem and I had wasted their life force. That morning at class, my teacher gave me my first compliment and hope that I would be able to eventually place on canvas my desired images. Happy about my accomplishment and saddened too for the life of my pearls, I realized probably for the first time in my life that there was an interaction between gems and myself. My pearls had given their love and life to me. Love from the sea had been so freely offered.

In my ring today lie three new gems, not pearls, but ruby red garnets to say a positive thank you to their former landlords for stimulating my career in the arts.

PERIDOT

Peridot is a transparent olive green magnesium iron silicate, sometimes called olivine. Peridots, however, can also be found in lemon yellow in some mines. These were called "topazoz" by the ancient Egyptians, like topaz for sun, as they believed they glowed in the dark like fire lanterns. Especially prized by the Egyptian pharaoh himself for his personal adornment, other peridots were used as curatives by the counsel priests to keep their minds free from envious thoughts and jealousies concerning the pharaoh's powers. As a medicinal stone, the peridot gem was often used for the healing of such physical problems as lack of muscle control and diseases of the liver. Many healers believed that these ailments would only respond to the curing effects of the sun. Thus peridot, like the topaz, had a direct identity placed on it as a gem containing the power of the sun.

In the Middle Ages, the peridot was given still another name, green chrysolite. This green stone was always set in gold to assure its full energy potential.

The alchemists believed that, in order for peridot to have the greatest effect against any dark vibrations, the stone had to be pierced and shaped into beads, then strung around the neck as a protective collar.

Thus, you could use peridots as your sun stones to prevent personal darkness from your fears and guilts. If you become depressed or fearful, a peridot can aid you in changing your attitude for it may just radiate the sun's energy as an additional resource to guide you.

The peridot is one of the few gemstones sometimes found in meteorites. It is interesting to note here that the ancients believed that peridots were ejected to earth by a sun's explosion. What a good example of how science and legend support each other in the historical folklore on the nature of gemstones!

Petrified Wood

PETRIFIED WOOD

Have you ever seen a trunk of branches of a tree that through time has turned to stone? This organic stone is petrified wood which has gone through a lengthy process of freezing, thawing and drying throughout thousands of years. You can see, especially in large pieces of petrified wood, the growth rings and the striated bands of trees that once lived millions of years ago. The stone wood family also includes petrified root or palm root which is found in many areas of the world where foliage at one time grew.

History has indiscriminately interwoven the legends and folklore of petrified wood with many agates, for the stones are very much alike in their banded physical properties. Since this stone was found plentifully in much of North America, it was utilized as talismans by many Indian medicine men who believed it offered protection against infections and bodily injuries. Petrified wood can be found in many pieces of ancient Indian jewelry. The Indians also used the stone woods as rubbing stones in ceremonies to call upon the elements of the earth.

Petrified woods can ground and secure you, and aid in preventing work stress. You can also use them to restore your physical energy. Most executive men and women would do well to have a piece of petrified wood on their desks. Petrified and agatized woods carved into bookends, clock faces, penholders and other ornamental objects make interesting desk pieces. If you are moving to a new location, a piece of petrified root might aid you as you begin to make new friends for it will help to ease some of your location fears.

Be physically strong, be secure at work, try an old tree turned to stone.

QUARTZ

Identifying the quartz family is both easy and difficult, as quartz is the most common earth mineral yet, like the agates, there are quartz agates and agatized quartz. Quartz comes in almost all colors and is one of the greatest energy stones, for quartz conducts energy of all kinds. The quartz that we will be mostly concerned with here are the semiprecious stones and not the minerals. Let's classify the families of quartz according to their colors and markings for easier identification.

ROSE QUARTZ

Often called pink quartz, rose quartz is one of the most common varieties of the quartz family. It has been valued since ancient Egypt, honored by the Tibetans, and used by the Orientals. Rose quartz is still one of the major ornamental carving stones from China. Once used as a beautification aid, facial masks of rose quartz have been found in the tombs of Egypt. The Romans, as well as the Egyptians, believed that rose quartz would prevent wrinkles and clear and encourage a beautiful complexion.

You might use some rose quartz jewelry to boost and build your image.

Because of its self-enhancement quality, a piece of pink quartz can be especially good if you have a weight problem. Even on an exercise or beautification program, try rose quartz, for it will greatly foster your personal self-acceptance. So when you want to lose the wrinkles of your past, put on your rose quartz to put you in the pink!

WHITE QUARTZ

White quartz, although not usually considered a gem, can be shaped into cabochon or faceted into jewelry beads. The Romans used it as a healing stone in bead form to reduce glandular swelling and fevers and for its energy property of draining off excesses. You might use a piece of white quartz for stimulation of your hopes and stabilization of your dreams. Try it as an attitude aid, and wear it for draining off any blocked areas that are preventing your dreams from coming true. In a piece of jewelry, this snowy white quartz can help you to use your own inner resources and potentials to alleviate your self-blocks. So dream away with security that your dreams will come true.

YELLOW QUARTZ

Yellow quartz, whose color is due to the presence of ferric iron, is often called citrine. Citrines, a common substitute in jewelry for topaz, are good gemstones to stimulate communications, since their energy reflects the yellow rays of the sun. This magnetic radiating energy can aid your voice projection, so why not make it a stone of choice for acting or performing? Yellow quartz, like other quartz, can be found just about anywhere and therefore is quite inexpensive to wear or collect. When you desire a strong physical image, or particularly when you want to project a dynamic positive image in communications, try a gem jewel of citrine quartz. Call it topaz for sun energy.

SMOKEY QUARTZ

Often identified as brown quartz, the color of smokey quartz appears to be caused by natural radioactivity in the stone's formation. This common gemstone is mined commercially in South America where it is then faceted into brilliant gems. Because of the perpetual energy contained within a smokey quartz, it can be a good stone to increase endurance, acting as an energy generator when you may need that extra little boost. Smokey quartz is nature's safe energy plant, as well as being beautiful in all forms of jewelry. A gem of brown energy power, use it to give you the strength of the earth.

RUTILATED QUARTZ

A fine-grained quartz, rutilated quartz appears as a clear quartz crystal with ribbons or threads of silver or gold running through it which may create a shooting star effect. A piece of rutilated quartz in your pocket can be a wonderful

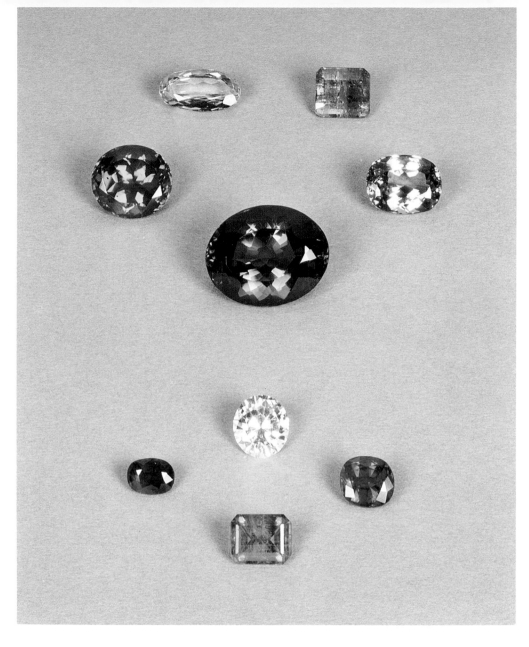

Aquamarine   *Tourmaline*

Peridot   *Topaz*

Amethyst

Diamond

Ruby   *Sapphire*

Emerald

stone for strengthening positive direction. This gold-lined quartz is like other energy generator stations, except it will also help to direct the energy positively outside of yourself. Rutilated quartz will also help keep your loved ones close to you in thought and feelings if you've become separated or out of contact with them. Always a good stone for those of you who may be lonely, its golden threads can lead you to love, goals, and in positive directions.

DRUZY QUARTZ

Druzy quartz is a popular specimen gem, composed of small bubbles of quartz resembling blown foam. It comes in a variety of colors: green, blue, purple, brown or pink, depending on the mineral associated with the crystals. The energy generated from the druzy stone depends a great deal upon the mineral contained within. Bright green druzy, for example, is found in small veins in mines of malachite and therefore offers the properties of malachite. Chrysocolla druzy, one of the most popular of the druzies because of its exquisite blue color, acts like an additional copper gemstone. Grape or violet druzy, nicknamed "passion purple" because of its cobalt mineral, acts as a soother and relaxer. The colors reflected through the druzy usually cause reactions similar to the psychological responses to color since druzy is actually only small crystals of quartz sending energy. For instance, blue calms the mind, violet supports the intuitive, and yellow or brown strengthens the body. Druzy quartz bubbles up the magnetic energy of the quartz and aids in the absorption of the combined minerals. Wear your druzy for a beautiful boost.

RHODOCHROSITE

Rhodochrosite is a pink translucent stone with a milky, lacy design visible within. This rose to rose-red stone becomes a marvel of beauty when cut into a cabochon.

There are few legends surrounding the rhodochrosite, also called Rosa del Inca or Inca rose, for it was primarily mined in very remote regions of Argentina. Discovered by the Incas, it was long treasured by them as a pink rosette pearl of great value, for rhodochrosites were often found as large nodules of mineral ore. Its name comes from the Greek words "rhodo" for rose and "cros" which means color. Colorado pink rhodochrosite in clean gems is very popular today and quite expensive.

A rescue/remedy stone, the pink rhodochrosite can rescue the rescuer, as well as the victim. It can be used to bring a new love into your life, to help you when searching for romance. You could say that a rhodochrosite can beautifully guide you in your quest for emotional happiness.

Rhodochrosites in crystal form, seldom faceted because of their delicacy, are often made into beads. They are stunningly beautiful when used as cabochons for jewelry settings. They vary from pale pink to deep raspberry red. Used in pink sweetheart rosettes as a rose to the rescue, a rhodochrosite helps restore balance to the psyche when it has been wounded by emotional or physical trauma.

Wear your rhodochrosite to enhance love of yourself and to put you in the pink.

RHODONITE

Another pink stone, rhodonite is considered more a mineral than a gemstone for it is usually found in ore bodies, particularly those which produce silver and manganese. This stone may often be stained with black lead or zinc sparkles, while other times it could contain veins of gold and even silver. When crafted as a cabochon it becomes a beautiful gem. Commonly found in the southwest United States, high quality rhodonite was frequently found in the ore dumps around silver mines.

Rhodonite's outstanding energy property is an aid to restoration of physical energy which has been drained due to emotional trauma/drama. It may reverse mineral depletion by providing additional strength because of its lead and mineral content as well as its pink color. Additionally, rhodonite promotes self-esteem, feelings of self-worth, and good self-confidence. If you need a moral boost, use a rhodonite as a gemstone lift.

RHYOLITE

Rhyolite, an opaque pink-to-brown stone, either banded or in rosette design, is also often found in highly mineralized areas. Purple striations sometimes found in rhyolite are because of the manganese. This stone is a favorite among rock hounds because of its magnificent bandings or rosette patternings. As hard as agate, rhyolite is sometimes mistaken for pink lace agate.

Like other pink stones, rhyolite can be a physical and emotional stabilizer. It acts less as a rescuer and more as a durable emotional support stone when an extra thrust for the expressions of your heart is needed. Rhyolite can help strengthen the permanency of a love relationship, or even stimulate emotional ardor. And because a happy romance produces a beautiful countenance, rhyolite is considered a physical rejuvenator. Since rhyolite is an earth gem associated with ores, it is best when set in silver.

Rhyolite can expand your love ties. Tie one on your finger.

ALL OF THE ABOVE ROSE STONES . . . RHODOCHROSITE, RHODONITE AND RHYOLITE . . . ARE DISTINCT EMOTIONAL AIDS. THEY ARE NOTED FOR THEIR POWER TO RESCUE, TO SUPPORT YOU, AND TO INCREASE YOUR SELF-RESPECT, SELF-WORTH AND HARMONY OF LOVE.

RUBY

The ruby, the most valuable of all gemstones, is a variety of corundum. It appears as a pinkish, medium to dark red mineral of crystalline limestones and dolomites that have metamorphosed. With the depletion of many present mines, especially in Burma, there is not an abundance of good quality rubies. A star ruby, from the same corundum family, is formed by inclusions of rutile crystals which produce a six-rayed star on the face of the gem. Considered one of the most perfect gemstones, the ruby can be beautifully cabochoned as well as faceted.

Honored in history as the King and Queen of gems, the ancients considered rubies the perfect wedding stones. Their association with love, marriage, balance and royalty has held fast throughout time. Ancient Egyptians honored the ruby for beauty and love, physical protection and good fortune. It was considered to be the greatest physical protector of all known gems. In Eastern legends, the ruby was seen as a spiritual stone representing beauty of the soul.

A ruby symbolized the sun, for it was believed to contain the bloodline of humanity. The Lord of gems, the Hindus believed it burned with its own fire from within, sometimes even able to boil water. The Greeks believed that the ruby, when carved and impressed on wax, could melt the wax. Its history has always been associated with high energy. The ruby protected health and wealth, controlled passions, and even warmed cold bodies, like an infrared light. To own a ruby assured its wearer of contentment, physical prosperity and peace. This sensitive stone, in addition, had a history of turning pale when its owner was in physical danger.

Today, the high energy ruby is valued as a most precious commodity in watchmaking as well as in medical instruments. This, of course, only increases the stone's value, for it raises its price to you, the person who merely wants a little ole ruby for its beauty. You can use the ruby as an expression of spiritual devotion, or of lasting love. You can use it as a high energy stone for physical beauty and protection. Let your ruby energize your spirit and aid your self-image of one who loves oneself.

SAPPHIRE

Your sapphire may be transparent or translucent and is usually a blue gemstone of high value. A variety of corundum, like the ruby, sapphires can be found in large sizes, especially in many Sri Lanka mines. Next to the diamond, the corundums are the hardest known gems, making them some of the best jewelry stones, for they are durable as well as scratch resistant. The deep azure or dark royal blue of the sapphire is due to the coloration of ferric iron or titanium, while other colors of sapphires such as pink, green or yellow come from other mineral compounds.

In all folklore sapphires are associated with the attraction of divine favor to their owners, and are mentioned in every religious history. The Buddhists believed that the sapphire favored devotion and spiritual enlightenment. In Christianity, sapphires were favored by bishops and cardinals as the symbol of divine wisdom. In the Old Testament, the sapphire received frequent mention for its relationship to a universal intelligence. It was honored as a stone of prophecy and wisdom and even called the philosopher's stone. A gem of the soul, the crystal-blue sapphire is one of the universal gems of history tying all religions together like an ecumenical council.

Those sapphires which display a six-rayed star or asterisk are called star sapphires. Their formation, like the star ruby, is due to inclusions of rutiles producing the six-rayed star on the face of the gem. One of the most famous and noted star sapphires is the Star of India, a stone of great religious significance. Star sapphires have often been called stones of great destiny. Some cultures believed that the three light bars which cross to form the six points on the surface of the gem represented faith, hope, and destiny or mission. If you have ever thought that from the time you were a child you were worth something and that you would like to help humanity, the star sapphire can help you hold that dream and possibly make it a reality. Use it as your gem of destiny! A star sapphire will bring out the best in you for it may just stimulate that universal spark which supports your dreams.

All sapphires, crystal or star, are gems of destiny. They can contribute to your mental clarity, your perception and your wisdom. Whether you are an executive, a theologian, a judge, or simply a person who seeks the truth, a blue sapphire will guide your way to the stars.

SARD

Sard, the general name for all unnamed clear agates, comes in every variety of colors from pink and yellow, to gray and brown. Their history is the history of the agate, although sards were not as preferred by the ancients as were the multi-colored agates. The grayish- or bluish-tone sard was often used as a stone of protection. Commonly, in folklore, sards were used to supplement the action of other agates, particularly agates used for healing. For example, folk history mentions sard as having the healing property of reducing and relaxing physical spasms and colic when worn on the body over the abdomen. Only sards in clear cool colors were considered effective.

The Indian agates, a common group of sards, are usually found in colors of orange to gray and brown. These sards were used most often as powerful protection stones. Worn around the neck as beads, sard was said to protect its wearer from outside negative attacks.

Generally, most clear agates found in any rock shop are from the sard family, but when banded they become banded agates, or if they have eyes, they become eye agates. When you may need a little extra protection in your life, include one of the sards in your rock bag. A bead necklace of sards is very attractive and will color-coordinate with most of your wardrobe as well as provide additional strength and protection on the job.

SARDONYX

Sardonyx is actually a banded onyx with layers of sard or chalcedony alternately in colors of red, black and white. The sardonyx gem was often used in the Middle Ages to banish grief and woe, as well as to bring about more control of the emotions to aid its wearer to become happier. You might call it a stone for self-focus. Associated with the power of eloquence, bashful lovers might use this stone to strengthen emotional confidence, which in turn can aid the expression of inner feelings. With this strengthening property, the sardonyx bands together people who are alike. You can use it to link with your loved one on an emotional level when you're having difficulty communicating.

While its buddy the onyx is a separator, the sardonyx is the binder and ties up loose ends and closes gaps. It will protect your household and your personal belongings, giving you feelings of material security. Carry one in your suitcase or pocketbook for it is a fine securer stone and will keep you protected. For all of you communicators, a sardonyx can be a marvelous support to obtain audience response and participation; in effect, to aid you to conquer your audience.

Tie up all your loose energies with your sardonyx.

SCARAB

The scarab, a carved beetle stone, has a history directly related to ancient Egypt. No other culture had such a historical connection to the scarab as the Egyptians, who honored the scarab beetle and named it scarabaeus sacer. The beetle, which rolled its food into a ball before eating, reminded those ancient philosophers of the rolling of the all-powerful sun across the sky. Thus, the scarab became the symbol of the sun god. The beetles, which normally lived underground, were believed to be reborn every day at noon when they came to the surface to take flight. It logically followed, then, for the Egyptians to symbolize the scarab as resurrection, flight and eternal life.

In ancient jewelry, the scarab was carved into many stones and gems, usually inscribed with a blessing to the person who was to wear it. To commemorate certain events, a seal was carved into the form of a scarab with the date and the event inscribed on the back.

Today, as in the past, we see scarabs carved in jade, agate, crystal, even bone and sandstone. The scarab itself represents identity and independence of one's beliefs. The scarab can support self-discovery as well as strengthen your faith since it may represent your personal resurrection.

Bracelets, earrings, or necklaces of scarab cuts usually contain a variety of gem and stone combinations which can be of equal importance. Your scarab gem pieces may contain the colors of red, yellow, green, blue, pink, and black.

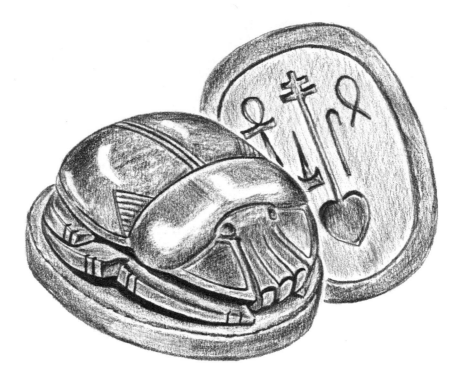

An example might be:

RED - Carnelian or Red Jasper
YELLOW - Tiger's Eye or Yellow Jasper
GREEN - Chrysophase or Jade
BLUE - Sodalite or Lapis Lazuli or Blue Chrysolite
PINK - Rhodonite or Rhodochrosite and sometimes Pink Jasper
BLACK - Black Onyx or Jet

Another example might be a jade scarab bracelet which would contain the spectrum of jade colors. Any scarab bracelet's charm is its ability to combine the various energies of color, the symbol, and the properties from the gemstones themselves. There are many possibilities for designing your own scarab bracelet. You can delight in fitting various stones with the listed colors to suit your particular needs. Scarabs assure self-identity, so wear a scarab to help you to find yourself.

SERPENTINE

Serpentine, a banded or grained agatized green rock commonly found in bedrock, is a choice carving rock. Its color ranges from light green to gray or even to a deep olive green. Historically, serpentine was used as a traveler's protection stone, particularly for traders who went from town to town, or sailors who went from port to port. The ancient Africans used it as a trading bead. Roman travelers wore it for night protection to keep away unseen dangers. North American Indians wore it with coral to secure their physical survival in harsh environments. Many carved serpentine amulets have been found in ancient tombs signifying transition stones, possibly to protect the tomb owner's soul in its journey through death. Serpentine talismans have been found carved into necklaces, prayer sticks, and inlaid into burial pots.

You can use serpentine as a good relocation stone when you are moving, for it can help to ensure your security and can divert unpleasant stresses or changes. You may also utilize it as a protector for your personal belongings in your home. The bands on the green serpentine will help to direct proper use of energy; thereby, the stone will act as a protector from outside intrusions. It is a wonderful stone to carve and place on your mantel like the "lion dogs" of old.

SODALITE

You might mistake sodalite, an opaque dark blue stone, for lazulite or lapis because of the basic color similarities. Again, because of its deep blue color and hardness, sodalite is constantly confused with the royal blue of lapis lazuli as well as the rich gray blue of turquoise. This identity crisis is compounded by its historical parallels with lapis and turquoise. In ancient tombs and ruins, sodalite has been discovered in places of ornamentation where lapis lazuli might have been expected. However, sodalite has its own personal identity.

Usually found in igneous rock in volcanic debris, sodalite comes from the core of the earth. It is a tough stone, yet easy to cabochon, like jasper. The color or crystalline variety of sodalite even lends itself to faceting in spite of its lack of transparency and mineral makeup. Beautiful objects can also be carved from this stone, for it does reflect some light through its stone body.

In history, sodalite was frequently used by Egyptian priests to dispel guilt and fears and to strengthen the power of mind over body. Most importantly, the properties of sodalite will provide a stone bridge between your subconscious and conscious mind, to connect your thoughts to your feelings, helping to eliminate guilt and fears better than any other stone. With a clear insightful mind you can find inner peace. Sodalite, although physically strikingly like lapis, will clear vision rather than stimulate wisdom and mind expansion. Use this blue stone as a lens to see the sky without clouds of fear and doubt.

SHELLS

Shells, like coral, are marine life and make wonderful organic jewelry. Shells are the houses or walls of water animals. Some of the most common shells used in personal jewelry are clam, conch, abalone, tortoiseshell, mother of pearl, and puca shells. Except for some tortoise shell, most have been nurtured under sea water, which gives them an oceanic and biological source of protection energy.

Shells can be found in every color of the rainbow, from the pearliest pink to iridescent abalone or even to the earth brown of the turtle. Shell beauty ornaments have been discovered in tombs of Egypt as well as in many ancient South American Indian diggings. Highly prized by the ancient tribes of American Indians, they were used not only for trade, but as displays of wealth when worn around the neck. They were some of the earliest monetary trading beads.

Folklore identifies shells with beauty, physical strength and power. Early Romans built their civilization by the sea, carving seashells into every form of objects of beautification, such as earrings, fans, hair combs and even eating utensils. These carvings often represented images of their gods and of their heroes. It was believed that the shell could bring to them the power of the carved image. Cameos, the most elegant carved expression for the shell, first represented gods and heroes. Later, this carved image merged into the head of a very feminine woman representing physical beauty.

You can use shells to improve your self-image, to help organize your life, and to increase your personal strength and endurance.

TOPAZ

Although you can find topaz in many colors, including yellow, blue, rose and brown, the range of yellow and brown are the most commercially important. Golden amber topaz has the highest market value and has been mined on many continents.

A very popular and durable transparent gem, topaz was identified as the "golden stone" or "fire stone" during its spectacular history. In the ancient language of the Hindus, topaz meant "fire." Ancient lore claims great healing powers for this stone, especially the power to control angry passions and to balance diseases of emotional origin. The earliest physician healers recognized that the topaz possessed outstanding magnetic energy and even in the Middle Ages, this gem was placed under the pillow at night to calm stress and to restore physical energy. It was also believed to prevent colds and tuberculosis because of its ability to give additional strength to the breathing mechanics of the body. Another legend states when topaz was hung around the neck it imparted strength to the intelligence while calming the emotions. Worn on the fingers, it was considered a protection stone against untimely or accidental death because of the belief that the topaz would lose its color in the presence of danger.

To the ancient Egyptians, the topaz symbolized Ra, the sun god, giver of life and fertility, and was, therefore, an extremely powerful energy gem. The topaz was the second most preferred stone in the breastplate of the Jewish high priest.

You can use your topaz to help you calm your emotions, relieve your tensions and stress and restore your physical energy. Since it is a stone that was thought to be good for colds, similar to coral, amber and citrine, and a natural protector from such, you can carry one in your pocket, as an extra vitamin C.

Citrine, a yellow quartz, a common substitute for gem topaz, though a slightly different crystalline form, has almost the same power as topaz. If you can't afford a true topaz, try a citrine for personal energy and wear it.

Both topaz and citrine, the color gems of the sun, can bring light and warmth into your life.

TOURMALINE

Tourmaline is a name applied to a family of aluminum silicate minerals mixed with various metals and usually found as crystals in granite rocks. Many appear as spike-like transparent stones in clear quartz deposits. These tourmaline crystals have electric and magnetic properties greater than those of the family of quartz crystals.

Tourmalines come in a huge variety of colors: green, pink, red, blue, brown, and black, due to their various mineral ingredients, and are frequently mixed in coloration, lengthwise or in cross sections. Even the name comes from the ancient Singhalese word, "turmali," meaning "a mixed-color precious stone." Their chemical compositions are so complex that John Ruskin noted in 1890 that "the chemistry of the tourmaline is more like a medieval doctor's prescription than the making of the respectable mineral."

The ancients, particularly the Romans, used these colorful stones for their relaxing properties of inducing tranquil sleep, for calming the mind and for producing a relaxed body.

Of all the many different colored tourmalines, the most popular is the watermelon tourmaline, which appears as a pink crystal with a green rind rim. This gem has a remarkable energy property, one that can transfer energy between two individuals who are important to each other. Compare watermelon tourmaline communication capability to a Dick Tracy two-way watch/radio. This energy transference is interesting to note, for in industry, tourmalines are highly valued as electrical tuning circuits to conduct television and radio frequencies. The stones are used for their durability since high frequencies can be passed through them and they will not shatter as do other crystals.

You can use tourmaline for super magnetic sending and receiving. When warmed or rubbed, it becomes charged with magnetic electricity and will act just like a magnet sending your thoughts out and attracting return energy.

There is another interesting variety of tourmaline known as "tourmalated quartz." This stone phenomenon occurs when little black tourmaline crystals, not yet formed into larger gemstones, are embedded in quartz rocks. The quartz appears threaded with small black projectiles. These stones make beautiful cabochons when polished. You can use the tourmalated quartz like a tourmaline, as an energy conductor or stimulant, to stimulate your direction, your achievement, or your positive action. A piece of tourmalated quartz can relax your mind, while shifting it into positive action.

Pink or rose tourmaline, favorites of the tourmaline family, can stimulate love and new friends. These rose stones promote personal love currents by flowing your love out to others and magnetically bringing it back to you. If you experience difficulty at first wearing a tourmaline, it may be due to its super high energy. Wear it in small doses or carry one and rub it for luck. Wish for your self-happiness to be fulfilled.

TURQUOISE

Turquoise is a hydrous copper aluminum sulfate found in every color of blue, greenish blue or deep green. The rich blues are due to the abundance of copper mineral while green turquoise has more aluminum.

One of the gemstones that bridges all cultures, turquoise is found from East to West, from the Far East to the Southwest United States. It has been prized by every culture including those of Egypt, Persia, Tibet, as well as the Aztecs and Incas of South America. In the East and Far East, it was honored as a lucky stone and from there it originally got its name as the "Turks' stone."

In the Orient, a turquoise ring was worn as a protector against all things evil. The Oriental proverb states: "Given by a loving hand it brings with it happiness and good fortune." However, the ring emitted protective energy only if the stone was given by an affectionate friend. Turquoise was also believed to restore clear vision to the mind when the thinking became muddled and thus, it ensured good fortune.

For the Indians of Mexico and the Southwestern United States, the turquoise was used to guard burial sites. The Indian priests wore it in ceremonies when calling upon the great spirit of the sky. Yet, part of its popularity was due to its easy accessibility in America. The stone was found close to the earth's surface and was easy to mine. Many of the Indian civilizations honored it as the universal stone, for they believed their minds would become one with the universe when wearing the turquoise. Because of the stone's ability to change color they used it to prophesy or to discover if a drought or other natural disaster was approaching. To the prehistoric Indian, turquoise, worn on the body or used in ceremonies, always signified the god of the sky alive in the earth, and in that way, it acted as a divining stone.

Legends claim that the turquoise changes color, losing its blue to become green when drained by a person wearing it or when it is used up. Except for the opal or the pearl, the turquoise is subject to a color change more than any other gem. If your turquoise loses its blue color, you may be in need of relaxation. There are some practical reasons for this assumption, as many studies have shown that sometimes there is an elevation of copper in the body when a person is under continual stress. The copper in the body's chemistry may have a direct association to the copper in the turquoise stone. One may interact with the other. The turquoise, a very soft and highly absorbent stone, may be one of the gemstones which shows a direct chemical reaction between a stone and the human body.

On the other hand, turquoise can relax your mind and ease mental tensions, calming your emotions and stress overstimulation. You can also use it as a protective self-love stone when you feel drained by worrisome people. Instead of saying, "No, leave me alone," wear a turquoise ring as your friendly protector.

ZIRCON

Commonly found in granite, zircons are relatively rare in gem quality. Yet, faceted, they rival the diamond in beauty. Zircon is a gem mineral used in determining the age of any rock because of its uranium composition. By counting the tracks of the decaying uranium in the zircon, one can determine how long ago the parent rock reached a temperature where the zircon could be formed.

Zircons can occur in square, prismatic crystals and are found in every color of the rainbow, such as blue, red, orange-yellow, green or brown or even clear like the diamond.

The zircon has been mentioned in the Bible and other ancient texts by many different names, mainly hyacinth, jacinth, and ligure, according to their color identity.

In the Middle Ages the yellow variety of zircons, ligure, was mainly used as a gem to increase satisfaction of physical desires. The orange variety, jacinth, called "the protector stone from Heaven," was used for safe passage for travelers and to assure the wearer a cordial reception wherever he went. When a person suffered emotional problems of the heart, jacinth was called upon to alleviate the agony and heal the pain. The brown/red variety, hyacinth, has a strong history of healing in many legends and folklore of zircon stones. It was usually used to calm the emotions, to produce sleep or to restore the appetite as well as to banish depression and melancholy.

Zircon is a magnificent stone which reflects a lot of light. It has the properties of the diamond to absorb energy and the crystal to express energy. It can absorb, hold and express. The healing properties have usually been associated with emotional/physical balance. When you feel emotionally upset, the zircon can become a wonderful stabilizer and balancer. Also it will be a good protector from outside angry attacks. When you feel threatened, put on your zircon. Like the crystal, it is a great all-around healer. When you see red, try the red, yellow or orange of the zircon to put you in the pink.

What Metal with What Stone

CHAPTER
8

8
What Metal with What Stone

Many persons continually ask what metal they should use to set their gemstones. They should consider the ore in which to set their stones in order to bring out the gems' best qualities.

When a gemstone is mounted in gold or silver, the metal will usually support the light or mineral contained within the particular gemstone in order to reinforce the gem's energy reaction. There are five major ores commonly used in jewelry. Three are precious metals: gold, silver, and platinum, and two are semiprecious metals: copper and brass.

Gold is by far the best energy conductor, be it white or yellow. Gold not only enhances a gem or stone, but it stimulates and activates the action of the stone like a dose of sun energy. Gold is preferred by most people, for it does not tarnish, it is extremely durable, and it reminds us of wealth and value. As you know, gold is very expensive, and this ore can help honor your gem, as well as you.

Silver has been known as the moon metal and is a stabilizer and securer of the action of the gemstone's energy. Like a mother to a stone, it does not expand the energy of the stone, but rather acts as an existing support to the stone's properties. Silver will reflect an individual's self-esteem and therefore can encourage the personality of the gemstone itself. Gems that are set in silver are supported with the silver ore energy rather than stimulated as with that of gold.

Platinum is the most precious metal and gems set in platinum must have a high energy or brilliance in order to cope with the intensity of the platinum. Rubies, emeralds, sapphires, diamonds and tourmalines are some of the stones whose energies are not disturbed by the platinum. Diamonds have a strong brilliance, rubies and tourmalines have high energy, and emeralds and sapphires have strong energy influence.

Copper acts as a conductor when worn on the body. It will aid the properties of the gem's minerals to react with the body. When combined with any gemstone high in copper content, it strengthens the copper reaction with the body. Copper jewelry can be extremely effective with malachite, turquoise, chrysocolla and azurite, which are all copper ore gemstones. Copper gives little support to stones that do not contain metals or ores. Yet, copper will enhance the action of silver or gold when combined with either metal in a piece of jewelry. The process of electroplating uses copper, nickel, and gold and this setting will support most gem specimens for beauty and energy.

Brass is often used as a substitute for gold. Brass, like copper, strengthens the physical reaction of gems to the body. Gems set or mounted in brass are supportive to the body due to the iron content in the composition of brass. Although brass is a delicate metal, it will hold stones securely. Many antique settings for jewelry were made from brass or bronze in order to bring out the rich colors of the gems.

Diamonds love to be set in gold or platinum. Earlier in the book we talked about diamonds having a high thermal energy and with this information we know that diamonds radiate light from their faceted surfaces, not from within. Therefore diamonds go well with the energy of gold or platinum, for the ores aid their brilliance. You might never think of setting a diamond in silver, yet this combination, especially with sapphires, can be very lovely. Amethyst is also very beautiful in silver, as silver supports its intuitive properties. Moonstones love silver settings, as silver is the ore of the moon.

On the other hand, there are certain stones that are better not set in silver settings or mountings, such as amber, for amber itself is a conductor of heat and energy. Another gem, tourmaline, needs an action ore such as gold or platinum to complete its power energy circuit. Zircon, a conductor of enormous amounts of energy, also needs one of these warm, strong ores. On the other hand, opals and fire agates, powerful energy stones, do well when set in silver. If an opal is too strong of an energy stone for you to wear, try setting it in silver. Most jaspers and agates do well in silver settings, as silver is a natural earth metal and combines easily with most earth stones.

Copper, as said before, can be used with copper stones, or mineral and high metal stones, such as tiger's eye and mica stones, aventurines and rhodonites. Copper is not the best setting for the crystalline stones, with the exception of amethyst, for copper, like silver, can support its intuitive properties. Pearls, fossils or corals do not work well in copper settings. This combination would detract from the organic properties of these biological gems. Gold and brass can usually be combined with all quartzes, corundums, or crystalline gems.

In jewelry designing there are, of course, some stones and gems that are better not combined in the same settings; for example, the mind relaxers and the mind stimulators do not mix well. When stones have counteractions, don't mix and match them in the same settings or in necklaces. For example, blue lace agate and lapis lazuli don't mix well because one relaxes the mind, and the other stimulates the mind. Amethyst and carnelian don't go together because carnelian secures the body and action and cancels out the power of the amethyst. Lapis lazuli and turquoise, again a stimulator and a relaxer, will not combine in their actions. Turquoise and malachite are another similar case. Malachite is a mental stimulator and protector, so the turquoise will cancel out the watchfulness of the malachite and put the malachite to sleep. Turquoise and diamond won't work either because their actions are not alike. Diamonds absorb all energy and can drain the calming effect of the turquoise.

Feel your gems, read about the gem energy, then combine them in settings that complement each other.

Ore and Stone Combinations

GOLD

ALL STONES

BRASS

ALL STONES

ALL AGATES
MOONSTONES
MINERAL STONES

SILVER

AMETHYST

DIAMONDS
EYE STONES
LAPIS LAZULI

No Amber, Tourmaline, Zircon.

COPPER STONES
TURQUOISE
CHRYSOCOLLA

COPPER

MICA STONES

AVENTURINE
RHODONITE
AMETHYST

SAPPHIRES
DIAMONDS
RUBIES

PLATINUM

EMERALDS

TOURMALINES
ZIRCONS
TOPAZ

All Precious Stones.

Alternative Ways
to Use Stones

CHAPTER
9

9
Alternative Ways to Use Stones

There are many ways to own and wear gems and stones without investing a lot of money. Gems or stones do not always have to be in the form of jewelry to be pleasing and functional. You can use and find gem specimens very inexpensively. While hiking or rockhounding, you can find beautiful mineral rocks, or specimens that attract you. Many gemstones are found in bedrock. Some are naturally polished from the elements while others can be found as crystalline spikes that you can break off. You can find others in creeks or river beds while vacationing in the mountains. At the seashore there is always a treasure of shells, fossils, and beautifully polished stones. These gemstones will become your "personal artifact stones," for they have been discovered by you. They belong to you for you to own.

On the other hand you can locate single bead stones, round, faceted, or in nugget form at gem stores and rock shops. They have been already shaped, and are usually drilled, and come in a variety of sizes. One bead gem may be all that you need to bring to you the vibration of your stone.

You can make your stones into jewelry or decorative objects. The results of your creativity can be very satisfying. You can create a beautiful object, or piece of jewelry, so as to have your special stones pass their energy on to you, while delighting your eyes at the same time.

Some suggestions for creative pursuits with your stones:

(a) Wrap them in wire as pendants to hang on your body, ears, as bracelets, in your car, or at home.

(b) Attach your stones with glue or adhesive to backing materials such as wood, metal plaques, table surfaces or baskets and place them around your working space.

(c) Carry them in your pocket in silk, leather, or cotton pouches. But remember some stones are soft and will scratch easily. You should not place them with the harder stones as they are too fragile for that type of use.

☆ ☆ ☆

REMEMBER

1. Commonalities of color and energy effect are important when creating personal jewelry.

2. The mineral energies of stones combine well in jewelry with the animal energies of leather, feathers and woods. Put your stones back with the other earth energies.

3. Try necklace cords of silk, cotton, leather, or metal wires, such as tiger tail, gold, silver, copper or metal alloys.

4. Use the right settings of metals for the most beneficial energy effect.

5. Wear your gemstones anywhere on your body.

6. Large stone specimens such as agates and petrified woods have practical decorative uses and can be utilized on your tables or desks as paper-weights or bookends or just for beauty.

7. Always select gems and stones that make you feel good, never ones that someone else forces you to wear.

8. Be beautiful or handsome with your million year old earth products.

Color Properties
of Gemstones

CHAPTER
10

10
Color Properties of Gemstones

Color is a vibrational form of energy and has an effect on you. Your gemstones absorb and reflect this color energy. As you become more familiar with your stones, it will become clearer as to why stones of the same gem family have different influences due to their individual colors. For example, you can compare the action of different colored quartzes, of different tourmalines, of any of the agates and corals. To help you see how color and gems go hand in hand in energy reaction, here is a general guide to color actions.

Red is a strong physical and emotional color. Generally, red gems and jaspers may be used for those of you who need additional physical energy. Red agates or red amber can be used by anyone to reduce shyness, weakness and physical sensitivities. Red corals influence support for the body and aid healing of respiratory infections. They also act as a good preventative for colds.

Pink is a nurturing and soothing color and is a wonderful color stone for self-rescue or self-enhancement. Pink stones, such as rhodochrosite and rhodonite, influence self-esteem, while rose quartz is always good to enhance your self-image. Pink pearls can promote your loving instincts while pink coral of the sea always supports a loving attitude.

Orange is an energy focused color and is very stimulating for motivation, goal and direction focusing as well as for promoting better organizational habits. Orange stones, particularly the carnelians, are good aids for training, for coordination of physical exercise programs, and for balancing body energy levels. Carnelians and Brazilian agates can be used as appetite stimulants for children and to prevent a listless attitude when you're not feeling as bubbly with energy as you want to.

Yellow is a communication color. Topaz, citrines and yellow zircons help to stimulate conversation, cheery attitudes, and one's ability to share. You can always depend upon yellow amber to prevent shyness, protect your sensitivity, or even as an aid to alleviate many old fears and guilt. A specimen of yellow quartz on your desk can aid in stimulation of better communication, open sharing, and honesty in work.

Green is the major balancing color and can act as an emotional soother. Most green gems and stones, such as malachite and chrysocolla, are wonderful aids to reduce mental confusion, even over-anxiety, and will react to some forms of hyperactivity. Bloodstone, the jasper energy mover, supports relaxation, calms hyperkinetic fatigue, and most importantly will soothe over-emotional reaction to stresses, internal and external.

Blue is the major intellectual and mind color. The lapis lazuli as a gemstone can promote creativity, mental control, and intellectual astuteness. The light blue lace agate is an agate to calm the mind while supporting creative inducement. Blue gems are very popular as they aid the mind. Another stone, dark blue sodalite or blue sardonyx, will aid intellectual independence. The rich blue sapphires can give self-assertiveness, even desires for higher goals as well as increase personal responsibility over one's life. All blue stones can be worn with red and yellow stones, for they pull the balance of the spectrum together. Dark blue sodalite set in jewelry with red coral stimulates independent physical activities while dark blue sapphires surrounded with yellow topaz can support independent communication and be a wonderful aid to public speakers.

Violet or *Purple* is the most sensitive and intuitive color. The gemstones of amethyst will open receptivity and introspection of one's mind or spirit. You who are extremely sensitive are encouraged not to wear your amethysts alone but wear other gems of yellow, green or dark blue along with your purple gemstone. The addition of these colors will balance and protect your sensitive nature, or control any mental fatigue. The Mexican lace agates, which have a violet hue, can act to secure you emotionally and to promote your inner happiness.

Brown is the basic security color. All brown agates, woods or jaspers can promote and influence security and give to you a feeling of ease and stability. Brown stones can also prevent fears and stresses, for they act as stabilizers to the emotions. Brown banded agates are particularly good for self-protection and inner security.

Black is the strongest disciplinary or protective color. Black stones such as jet, onyx and obsidian strengthen, protect and support any image of authority. The black stones will fortify other color gems such as diamond, but are not recommended for a child under the age of ten. Black gemstones always combine easily with the other multicolored gems such as pearls, moonstones and diamonds to offer protection to sensitive personalities. Wear these black beauties to keep invading or intruding energies out of your space.

Gems and Stones as Professional Image Supports

CHAPTER
11

11
Gems and Stones as Professional Image Supports

Another contribution of stone power, derived from the ancient lore of gemstones, is the energy-enhancing aid for job support. Certain stones can add that extra something to help your endurance levels, or give extra protection on the job. For example, in ancient Egypt, the master builders wore the carnelian breast-plate to signify their profession. Did the carnelian also have the power to support their creative design abilities? The rose quartz has a history of enhancing physical beauty, so could it not aid the beauty counselor of today? The lapis lazuli supported the wisdom of past leaders, could it not then enhance the executive who wants to make wise decisions? In the following charts, look up your work role or profession and maybe you'll find a stone that can offer you that extra support.

PROFESSION	GEMSTONE	PURPOSE
ACCOUNTANTS	Turquoise	aids mental relaxation
	Chrysocolla	calms emotional stress
	Red Jasper	supports physical endurance
ACTORS	Topaz	aids energy projection for communication
	Red Jasper	promotes sensitivity to audiences
	Brazilian Agate	increases physical stamina
AIRPLANE and AIRLINE WORKERS	Dendritic Agate	offers protection to travel
	Fire Agate	provides a safeguard over water
	Malachite	protects against accidents
ARCHEOLOGISTS and HISTORIANS	Sapphire	improves awareness of higher principles
	Lapis Lazuli	supports intellectual analysis
	Shells	encourages physical and historical organization
ARCHITECTS	Carnelian	creates a master building
	Crystal	provides a sensor to light and form
ARTISTS	Moonstones	increases self-love for improved self-expression
	Agates	stabilizes the imagination and inspiration
	Amethyst	stimulates intuitive abilities
	Crystal	serves as the Universal Art Stone which reflects the rainbow

PROFESSION	GEMSTONE	PURPOSE
ATHLETES	Petrified Wood & Ivory	increases physical stamina
	Carnelian	stimulates power
BANKERS	Diamond	reflects richness and self-satisfaction
	Aventurine	increases financial opportunity
BEAUTY CONSULTANTS	Rose Quartz	enhances self-image
	Rhodochrosite	promotes self-love
	Crystal	promotes self-expression
BUILDERS and CONSTRUCTION WORKERS	Carnelian	supports organization of form
	Banded Agate	gives direction; or protection from falling objects
	Shells & Ivory	improves personal organization
CHEFS, BAKERS, and COOKS	Agates	aids personal security
	Moss Agate & Plume Agate	promotes sensitivity to food products
COMPUTER OPERATORS	Turquoise	aids mental relaxation
	Chrysocolla	calms emotional stress
	Red Jasper	supports physical endurance
COUNSELORS	Crystal	enhances clear communications
	Bloodstone	regulates energy flow
DANCERS	Agates	strengthens the physical body
	Moonstone & Opal	encourages self-expression
DENTISTS	Fossils	influences teeth and mouth wholeness
	Agates	balances physical endurance
DETECTIVES	Tiger's Eye	stimulates clear sight and insight
	Zircon	aids in organization of facts
DIVERS and WATER WORKERS	Aquamarine	protects in water
	Tiger's Eye	provides underwater sight
DOCTORS and HEALERS	Jade	aids practical diagnosis
	Bloodstone	regulates energy flow
	Emerald	stimulates clear vision or insight
	Crystal	stimulates warmth
DRESSMAKERS	Chrysoberyls	prevents eye strain
	Pearl	increases patience

PROFESSION	GEMSTONE	PURPOSE
EDUCATORS	Geode	encourages professional freedom
	Agates	secures emotional endurance
	Moonstone	supports sharing activities
	Jade	stimulates practical applications
ELECTRICIANS	Red Jasper	ensures alertness
	Botswana Agate	protects and regulates energy
	Fire Agate	ensures protection around high energy
ENVIRONMEN-TALISTS	Emerald	encourages future sight
	Fossils	strengthens hindsight
	Agate	increases physical endurance
EXECUTIVES	Sapphire & Lapis Lazuli	stimulates the mind and increases wisdom
	Moonstone	inspires the heart and feeling
	Blue Lace Agate	tranquilizes and relaxes the mind
FARMERS	Agates & Petrified Wood	relaxes work burdens
	Obsidian	supports emotional endurance
GOVERNMENT WORKERS	Carnelian & Citrine	increases productivity
	Topaz & Smokey Quartz	improves interactions
HOUSEWIVES	Shells	promotes household organization
	Lace Agates	stimulates contentment with one's work
	Abalone	prevents fatigue
	Zircon	releases over-burdening of responsibilities
INVENTORS	Lapis Lazuli	increases new ideas
	Crystal	encourages inspiration
	Chrysocolla	relaxes the mind
JOURNALISTS	Sapphire	increases discernment
	Lapis Lazuli	promotes good judgment
	Carnelian	establishes form and organization
LABORERS	Turquoise	protects from bodily harm
	Red Coral	increases physical endurance
LAWYERS	Lapis Lazuli	aids in problem solving
	Sapphire	encourages good judgment

PROFESSION	GEMSTONE	PURPOSE
MILITARY PERSONNEL	Red Jasper	encourages emotional stability
	Carnelian	improves physical stamina
	Carved Jade	uplifts (when carved in the form of a faith symbol)
MINERS	Tourmaline	increases mental awareness
	Malachite	protects from unexplained accidents
MINISTERS	Amethyst	increases spiritual clarity
	Sapphire	supports wisdom and good judgment
MUSICIANS	Crystal	increases sensitivity to tonal vibrations
	Opal	opens sensitivity to audiences
	Pink Clamshell	re-energizes the physical
NURSES	Emerald	increases insight
	Bloodstone	regulates energy flow
	Jade	aids practical application
POLICE	Banded Agate	protects from attack
	Rhodochrosite	rescues the rescuer
	Red Jasper	aids physical endurance
POSTAL WORKERS	Speckled Agate & Dendritic Agate	protects travelers
	Blue Lace Agate	calms stress
PSYCHOLOGISTS	Moonstone	increases sensitivity to others
	Lapis Lazuli	promotes wisdom and good judgment
RADIO and TV WORKERS	Topaz & Citrine	energizes clearer communication
	Turquoise	releases anxiety
	Crystal	increases vocal vibrations
RECREATIONAL WORKERS	Agates	supports and increased physical and emotional endurance
	Topaz & Citrine	improves interactions
SALESPERSONS	Brazilian Agates	increases physical stamina
	Carnelian	stimulates motivation
	Topaz & Citrine	aids energy for communication
	Petrified Wood	relaxes mental stress

PROFESSION	GEMSTONE	PURPOSE
SECRETARIES	Malachite	stimulates clear thinking
	Moonstone	promotes sensitivity
	Red Jasper	provides extra patience
	Dendritic Agates	stabilizes energy levels
SINGERS	Red Coral	strengthens the voice
	Zircon	increases vocal projection
TELEPHONE WORKERS	Banded Agates	protects around electro-magnetic energy
	Tourmaline	sharpens mental accuracy
	Red Jasper	supports physical stamina
TRUCK and TAXI DRIVERS	Rutilated Quartz	guides direction
	Speckled Agate	protects travelers
VETERINARIANS	Jade	promotes practical healing
	Bloodstone	regulates energy flow
	Moss Agate	detoxifies body energies
	Ivory	protects from animal injuries
WAITRESSES and WAITERS	Rhodonite	rescues the self-image
	Red Jasper	increases physical endurance
	Moonstone	enhances self-acceptance
WRITERS	Sapphire	increases wisdom and knowledge
	Lapis Lazuli	improves intelligence
	Sodalite	removes mental confusion

Gem Energy Problem Solving Capabilities

CHAPTER 12

12
Gem Energy Problem Solving Capabilities

Have you ever thought of enlisting a stone to help you solve your problems? Your stones can serve as much as your energy makeup will accept their service, but your gemstones don't have power on their own to become problem solvers alone. They need interaction with you to perform each necessary function. Wear them, rub them, wish on them, and enjoy the amazing results they can bring to you.

Stones will aid, encourage, soothe, and support. Some can insure, strengthen, protect, and act efficiently as opportunity stones. Some may perform as inspirers which can serve you as good performance aids and ego boosters.

GEMSTONE	PROBLEM TO SOLVE
AGATE: Banded	Lack of strength or courage
Botswana	Uncertainty of personal direction
Indian	Emotional insecurity
Lace	Despair or depression
Moss	Clearing of toxicity
Plume	Fear of the unknown
Speckled	Extra protection to travelers
ALEXANDRITE	Not enough love of life
AMAZONITE	Loneliness
AMBER	Overwhelming stresses
AMETHYST	Lack of intuitive awareness
AQUAMARINE	Safety in marine travel
AVENTURINE	Lack of new opportunities
AZURITE	Mental dullness
BLOODSTONE (Heliotrope)	Energy blocks and limitation
BONE and IVORY	Need for extra spiritual & physical protection
CARNELIAN	Lack of energy to manifest
CAT'S EYE/TIGER'S EYE	Inability to see clearly
CHALCEDONY	Emotional lethargy
CHRYSOCOLLA	Emotional confusion

GEMSTONE	PROBLEM TO SOLVE
CORAL (all colors)	Lack of physical stamina
CRYSTAL	Bad habits
DIAMOND	Material insecurities
EMERALD	Lack of perception and inner clarity
GARNET	Intolerance and lack of popularity
GEODES	Dependencies on others
JADE	Lack of practicality

JASPER: Red
         Brown
         Green
	Lack of physical energy
	Lack of personal security
	Severe emotional stresses

JET	Emotional over-involvement
LAPIS LAZULI	Inability to accept leadership
MALACHITE	Lack of inner peace
MOONSTONE	Insensitivity to self and others
OBSIDIAN	Super-sensitivity to the environment
ONYX	Need for protection from outside influences
OPAL	Inability to share love
PEARL	Inability to nurture others
PERIDOT	Over-responsiveness to emotional stresses
PETRIFIED WOOD	Insecurity and uncertainty
QUARTZ	Feelings of unwantedness or rejection
DRUZY QUARTZ	Lack of clear insight
ROSE QUARTZ	Poor self-image
RUTILATED QUARTZ	Negative thoughts
SMOKEY QUARTZ	Lack of emotional support
WHITE QUARTZ	Decreased self-worth
YELLOW QUARTZ	Lack of open communications
RHODOCHROSITE	Emotional trauma
RHODONITE	Lack of self-acceptance

GEMSTONE	PROBLEM TO SOLVE
RHYOLITE	Feelings of continuous victimization
RUBY	Fear of being ugly and unloved
SAPPHIRE	Lack of better goal opportunities
SARD	Emotional insecurity concerning involvements
SARDONYX	Invasion from outside influences
SCARAB	Identity crisis
SERPENTINE	Lack of emotional stability
SHELLS	Lack of vitality
SODALITE	Guilty conscience
TOPAZ	Feelings of anger
TOURMALINE	Fear of accomplishment or success
TURQUOISE	Worry and mental confusion
ZIRCON	Feelings of negativity or frustrations

Gems and Stones
as Performance Aids

CHAPTER
13

13
Gems and Stones as Performance Aids

Protection, safety, detrimental habit release, or professional advancement are all positive performance uses for gemstones. The aquamarine aided the Romans traveling on water, while the turquoise aided the American Indian to get in touch with spirit. Use a gemstone as a performance support to help you reach one of your goals.

TO DEVELOP SPIRITUAL ABILITIES:

AMETHYST	for intuitive awareness
LAPIS LAZULI	for wisdom and truth
MOONSTONE	for humanitarian love and sensitivity
OPAL	for humanitarian love and service

TO BREAK DETRIMENTAL HABITS SUCH AS SMOKING OR DRINKING:

CRYSTALS, QUARTZ, and MAJOR ORES

TO PROTECT TRAVELERS FROM BODILY HARM:

AQUAMARINE	for marine travel
DENDRITE & SPECKLED AGATE	for air travel
DENDRITE, SPECKLED AGATE, & INDIA AGATE	for car travel

FOR SAFETY IN THE OPERATION OF MACHINERY:

JASPERS

FOR EFFICIENCY IN HOUSEHOLD MANAGEMENT:

SEASHELLS, FOSSILS, CORAL, and PETRIFIED WOODS

FOR PRODUCTIVITY AND FOR CAREER AND PROFESSIONAL ADVANCEMENT:

AGATES	for physical and emotional balance
EMERALDS	for creativity and problem solving
RUBIES	for mental balance
SAPPHIRES	for goal orientation and motivation

**FOR SOCIAL AND COMPETITIVE INTERACTION; TO STIMULATE
GOOD HUMOR AND TO AID RELAXATION:**

CHRYSOCOLLA   for mental relaxation
GREEN JADE   for practicality and wisdom
SODALITE   for release of subconscious fears and guilts
TURQUOISE   for inner joy and peace

Gems and Stones as Attitude Balancing Aids

CHAPTER
14

14
Gems and Stones as Attitude Balancing Aids

Energy from gems and stones, like colors, can positively affect our attitudes and give us emotional support. Listed alphabetically below are the common stones and their attitude balancing focus for aiding oneself.

AGATES	relate to the physical and emotional attitudes
Banded	attracts strength and courage
Blue Lace	offers emotional tranquility
Carnelian	provides and increases protection and endurance
Dendrite	the traveler's stone, aids security and endurance
Eye	counteracts negative thinking
India	offsets physical and emotional weakness
Lace	stimulates happiness
Moss-green	balances discordant emotional energies
Moss-red	increases physical stamina
Plume	decreases fear in job hunting or direction finding
Speckled	is another traveler's stone
ALEXANDRITE	stimulates sexual gratification and love of life
AMAZONITE	encourages faith and hope
AMBER	lifts the spirits
AMETHYST	stimulates intuitive awareness
AQUAMARINE	aids in marine travel and calms nervous tension
AVENTURINE	stimulates opportunity and motivation
BLOODSTONE	removes emotional blockages and limitations
CAT'S EYE and TIGER'S EYE	stimulate clear thinking and discernment; offer psychic protection
COPPER STONES and GEMS	
Azurite	stimulates mental powers
Chrysocolla	calms emotional stress
Malachite	stimulates mind power
Turquoise	aids mental relaxation and calms emotions
CORAL	promotes a sense of well-being

CRYSTALS	elevate thoughts, release bad habits, combat negativity and promote good habits
Pink Quartz	increases feeling of self-worth
Yellow Quartz or Citrine	expands mental clarity
DIAMOND	reflects light and thought, both positive and negative
EMERALD	stimulates truth and perception; promotes creativity
GARNET	decreases willfulness
GREEN JADE	stimulates practicality and wisdom
IVORY	promotes spiritual protection
JASPERS	
Brown	gives emotional security
Green	promotes a positive mental attitude
Red	protects against external stresses
JET	prevents deep depression
LAPIS LAZULI	stimulates wisdom and truthfulness
MOONSTONE	refines and stimulates all the senses; promotes unselfishness; called the humanitarian stone
OBSIDIAN	the Apache tear, provides protection for the super-sensitive
ONYX & SARDONYX	stimulate self-control and protection
OPAL	promotes psychic stability and the capacity to share
PEARL	stimulates feminine and material qualities
PERIDOT	balances physical energies to ward off emotional stress
PETRIFIED WOOD	gives emotional security
RHODOCHROSITE	a love rescue stone, balances trauma and stimulates forgiveness
RHODONITE	promotes self-assuredness
RHYOLITE	alleviates emotional stress
RUBY	protects sensitive natures and prevents schizophrenic attitudes
SAPPHIRE	relieves mental depression, promotes peace and happiness, and stimulates motivation and goal orientation

SHELLS	increases domestic organization and efficiency
SODALITE	dispels guilt
TOPAZ	calms the emotions and protects against external stresses
TOURMALINE	promotes attitudes of success and accomplishment
ZIRCON	reduces emotional negativity and promotes positive attitudes

THE THREE MAJOR
  ORES

Copper	prevents a negative attitude
Gold	promotes self-acceptance and self-enhancement
Silver	promotes self-improvement

Preferred Gems of the Ancients

CHAPTER
15

15
Preferred Gems of the Ancients

Back to the earliest traceable societies, gems were worn on the body only by rulers and members of the royal families. Later, with the growth of religion and out of respect for divine law and its earthly administration, priests, wise men and other religious leaders followed their monarchic leaders in adorning their bodies and their robes.

Necklaces were the first fashionable ornaments. Then came rings and earrings. Much later, broaches and pins came into wide usage. Crowns, face masks and facial jewelry were used to decorate noses, foreheads, mouths and cheeks. Such adornments have been discovered in tombs around the world, testifying to early man's preference for and appreciation of gems and stones.

The favored stones of societies, as diversified as their geographical locations, were:

EARLY EGYPTIANS	BABYLONIANS and MESOPOTAMIANS	EARLY JEWS
Agate	Amethyst	Agate
Amber	Carnelian	Amber
Azurite	Emerald	Amethyst
Carnelian	Garnet	Aquamarine
Chrysoberyl	Jasper	Diamond
Coral	Ruby	Emerald
Garnet	Sapphire	Garnet
Jade	Topaz - yellow	Jasper
Jasper		Onyx
Lapis Lazuli		Sardonyx
Malachite		Sapphire
Onyx		Topaz
Pearl		
Turquoise		

ROMANS	INCANS and MAYANS
Agate - all varieties	Agate
Amethyst	Coral
Aquamarine	Emerald
Emerald	Jade
Garnet	Jet
Lapis	Pipestone
Moonstone	Onyx
Ruby	Sardonyx
All Metals	Shells
	Turquoise

A Note From the Author

We hope that you have enjoyed exploring the unseen energy world of gems and stones. Many great minds and healers have contributed to this practical source of information. Experience now for yourself how the energy qualities of the gemstone kingdom can be supportive to your self-improvement. As humankind continues to develop greater sensitivity to its environment, gems and stones will once again be honored as planetary resources for energy and life. Since we continue to exist as divine composites of the animal, vegetable and mineral kingdoms we must interact more and come closer together to maintain our harmony and balance.

Feel free to use the following pages for listing your desires and wishes. Look up the stones that can best support you to obtain your goals. Keep a journal of your own "stone power" resources. Jot down your personal gem "family tree."

If you would like to share some of your experiences with us concerning personal reactions with gems or stones, or if you have any difficulty finding any of the gems and stones in this book, write to me, the author, c/o Domel Inc., P.O. Box 3829, Albuquerque, NM 87190. I always enjoy hearing how the stone world helps and supports the human family, and will be delighted to help you get in contact with your stone.

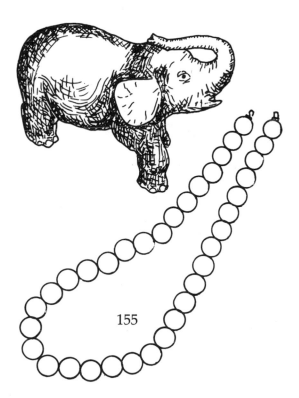

155

NOTES

NOTES

NOTES

NOTES

NOTES

NOTES

NOTES

NOTES

References

1. *A Field Guide in Color to Minerals, Rocks, and Precious Stones*, by Dr. Jaroslav Bauer, Octopus Books Limited, London, England.

2. *Amulets and Birthstones*, by Ivy A. BannermanPhillips, Llewellyn Publications Ltd., Los Angeles, CA.

3. *The Occult and Curative Powers of Precious Stones*, by William T. Fernie, M.D., Harper & Row Publications, New York, NY.

4. *The Curious Lore of Precious Stones*, by George Frederick Kunz, Dover Publications, Inc., Mineola, NY.

5. *Healing Stones*, by Doris M. Hodges, Pyramid Publishing, Perry, IA.

6. *Complete Color Prescription*, by Roland T. Hunt, Paramount Press, Los Angeles, CA.

7. *The Magic and Science of Jewels and Stones*, by Isadore Kozminsky, Finch Publishers, Ann Arbor, MI.

8. *Gems and Stones*, A.R.E. Press, Virginia Beach, VA.

9. *Twenty-two Gems, Stones, and Metals*, A.R.E. Press, Virginia Beach, VA.

10. *Precious Stones*, by W. B. Crow, Ph.D., Samuel Weiser, Inc., York Beach, ME.

11. *The Egyptian Book of the Dead*, by E. A. Wallis Budge, Dover Publications, Mineola, NY.

12. *The Mummy*, by E. A. Wallis Budge, Biblo & Tanner Booksellers, Cheshire, CT.

13. *Birthstones*, by Willard A. Heaps, Hawthorn Inc., New York, NY.

14. *Color Encyclopedia of Gemstones*, by Joel E. Arem, Ph.D., F.G.A., Van Nostrand Reinhold Company, New York, NY.

Note: Some of the above titles are out of print and in that case can only be found in personal, public, and other reference libraries.